LETTERS FROM COUNTRY LIFE

ALSO AVAILABLE FROM ECLIPSE PRESS

Affirmed and Alydar: Racing's Greatest Rivalry

At the Wire: Horse Racing's Greatest Moments, Updated Edition

Duel for the Crown: Affirmed, Alydar, and Racing's Greatest Rivalry

The First Kentucky Derby: Thirteen Black Jockeys, One Shady Owner, and the Little Red Horse That Wasn't Supposed to Win

Great Horse Racing Mysteries: True Tales from the Track, Updated Edition

Kelso: Racing's Five-Time Horse of the Year

The Kingmaker: How Northern Dancer Founded a Racing Dynasty, Updated Edition

Letters from Country Life: Adolphe Pons, Man o' War, and the Founding of Maryland's Oldest Thoroughbred Farm

Man o' War: Racehorse of the Century

Merryland: Two Years in the Life of a Racing Stable, Updated Edition

Ride of Their Lives: The Triumphs and Turmoil of Racing's Top Jockeys, Updated Edition

The Seabiscuit Story: From the Pages of the Nation's Most Prominent Racing Magazine

Seattle Slew: Racing's Only Undefeated Triple Crown Winner

Secretariat: Racing's Greatest Triple Crown Winner, 50th Anniversary Edition

Tales from the Triple Crown

The 10 Best Kentucky Derbies

War Admiral: Man o' War's Greatest Son

Women in Racing: In Their Own Words, Updated Edition

LETTERS FROM COUNTRY LIFE

Adolphe Pons, Man o' War, and the Founding of Maryland's Oldest Thoroughbred Farm

JOSH PONS
Two-Time Eclipse Award Winner

Foreword by Evan Hammonds
Former Editor, *BloodHorse* Magazine

Essex, Connecticut

An imprint of Globe Pequot, the trade division of
The Rowman & Littlefield Publishing Group, Inc.
4501 Forbes Boulevard, Suite 200,
Lanham, Maryland 20706
www.rowman.com

Distributed by NATIONAL BOOK NETWORK

Cover photos (left to right): Man o' War's mother, Mahubah, posed by Nursery Stud manager Elizabeth Kane in 1922; 1885 Plat Survey of Rockland Farm, renamed Country Life Farm in 1933; Adolphe A. Pons in 1933, beside Winters Run.

British Library Cataloguing in Publication Information Available

Library of Congress Cataloging-in-Publication Data

Names: Pons, Josh, author. | Hammonds, Evan, writer of foreword.
Title: Letters from Country Life : Adolphe Pons, Man o' War, and the founding of Maryland's oldest thoroughbred farm / Josh Pons ; foreword by Evan Hammonds.
Description: Essex, Connecticut : Eclipse Press, [2024]
Identifiers: LCCN 2024005731 (print) | LCCN 2024005732 (ebook) | ISBN 9781493081394 (trade paperback) | ISBN 9781493081400 (epub)
Subjects: LCSH: Country Life Farm (Bel Air, Harford County, Md.) | Horse farms—Maryland—Bel Air (Harford County)—History. | Horse breeder—Maryland—Bel Air (Harford County)—History.
Classification: LCC SF290.U6 P63 2024 (print) | LCC SF290.U6 (ebook) | DDC 636.1009752/74—dc23/eng/20240425
LC record available at https://lccn.loc.gov/2024005731
LC ebook record available at https://lccn.loc.gov/2024005732

∞™ The paper used in this publication meets the minimum requirements of American National Standard for Information Sciences—Permanence of Paper for Printed Library Materials, ANSI/NISO Z39.48-1992.

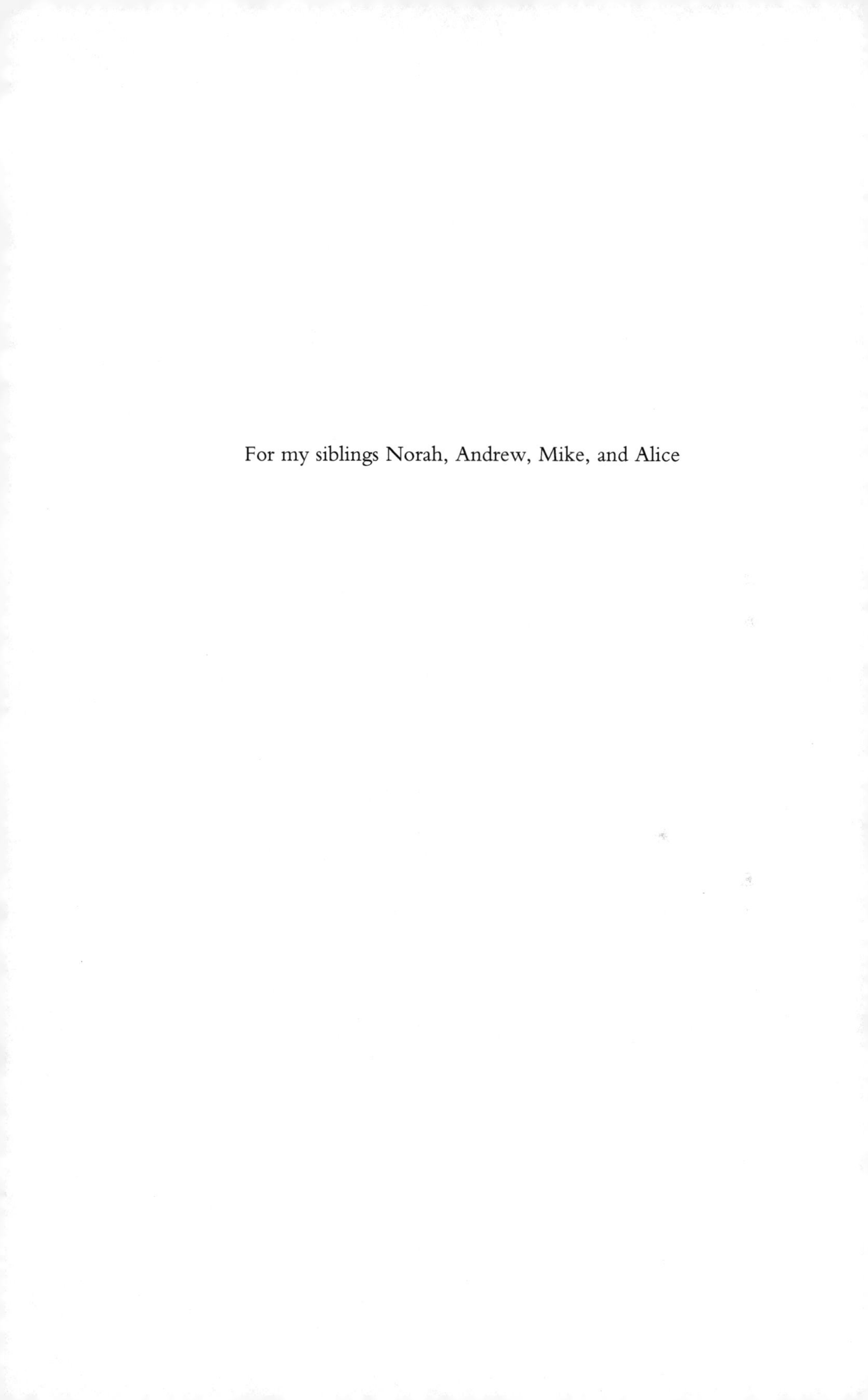

For my siblings Norah, Andrew, Mike, and Alice

There is no intention of making the claim
that the properties of a single ancestor
who lived so long ago
is strongly evident in descendants.

Yet, there is undoubtedly an influence
of all ancestors
no matter how far removed.

—John F. Wall, retired colonel of cavalry,
A Horseman's Handbook, 1939

She'll wish there was more,
and that's the great art o' letter-writin'.

—Charles Dickens, *Pickwick Papers*

CONTENTS

FOREWORD

How many times can lightning strike the same spot? If one happens to work at *BloodHorse* Publications, the answer is three. That is the number of times Maryland Thoroughbred horseman Josh Pons has approached the company with an idea, and the number of times editors, including myself, have taken the bait.

Not only have each of his columns been a hit in the weekly (now monthly) magazine, but also all three had additional wind in their sails in book form. The latest, *Letters from Country Life* (a.k.a. the "Letters from Rockland Farm" column), is in your hands.

Pons and his wife, Ellen, operate Country Life Farm near Bel Air, Maryland, along with his brother, Mike, and Mike's wife, Lisa. I first met Josh longer ago than either one of us care to remember, when he was working his way through law school at the University of Kentucky under venerable editor-in-chief Kent Hollingsworth and I was a high school senior lucky enough to land a part-time position at the magazine. It has been a friendship—and semi-working relationship—for nearly a half-century. I hope the relationship has been half as rewarding for him as it has been for me.

Pons's deft reporting skills landed him the Eclipse Award (racing's highest honor) for magazine writing in 1981. He later proved to be no one-hit wonder.

However, the young Pons soon left *BloodHorse* to return to Country Life Farm, where the family business has managed to bob and weave its way through a myriad of hurdles that have faced the Maryland Thoroughbred community through the decades. Luckily for us, he never lost his itch for writing; his byline returned in 1989 and appeared monthly through 1991 in serial format. *Country Life Diary* followed the daily life of the farm, and with Pons's ability to turn a phrase, it, too, won the Eclipse Award for journalism in 1992. Published in book form, it proved quite popular and one of the rare books about horses that required a reprint.

Pons called again a few years later, pitching a diary series dubbed "Merryland," which appeared in *BloodHorse* starting in March 2005. The series took readers through the Pons family's purchase of nearby Merryland Farm, a training center, in 2001, and offered a look at a different phase in the Thoroughbred life cycle: that of transforming a young horse into an equine athlete. It was no surprise when the popular series found its way to book form as well.

So, when Josh rang up *BloodHorse* in late 2017, there was no hesitation in my voice to agree to his latest pitch: to forensically deconstruct the boxes of his grandfather's correspondence Josh had found in the attic and basement of the farm's main house. His grandfather, Adolphe Pons, had purchased Rockland Farm in 1933 and renamed it Country Life Farm. Apparently, Adolphe kept everything, and his grandson has been constantly amazed at what has been slowly unboxed over the last few years.

Dubbed "the garret," the attic where Josh writes has since been transformed into a staging area for his research, a sanctuary of folding tables filled with musty books and farm paperwork, his mother's old big-band-era albums, and today's Americana music. It is a magical space.

Adolphe had earlier been the able-bodied personal secretary to Thoroughbred scion August Belmont II. Belmont, a larger-than-life character, was an important player in the formative years of the twentieth century in the United States, and as a Thoroughbred leader, bred the mighty Man o' War. Decades later, when Josh found unpublished photographic negatives of Big Red, he was quick to share his joy, and we promptly arranged a cover story with his newfound treasure.

Josh has many talents, and showed a new facet as historian, with his ability to take a box of ninety-year-old farm records and make them not only come alive but tie the generations together with what has been happening in the business during this century.

Pons is the rare bird—adept at the end of a shank or in front of a keyboard. And Ellen is equally impressive in her work behind the camera. Photographing farm life takes patience, and she has that in spades, as well as a cultured eye that adds colorful notes of realism, still-life, and impressionism to her husband's prose.

Whereas *Country Life Diary* was more about the day-to-day farm operation, filled with self-deprecating humor, *Letters from Country Life* is more introspective, filled with his family's story and how it has intertwined with the history of Thoroughbred racing in America, and its relevance to today. I'm sure you will agree it is a great read.

Evan Hammonds
Former Editor, *BloodHorse*
August 2024

AUTHOR'S NOTE

Every writer imitates some other writer they admire, at first. That's how I started this project—in imitation of journalist Margaret Aldrich's book *A Hilltop on the Marne: Being Letters Written June 3–Sept. 8, 1914.* She sent letters to an unnamed friend in America a century ago. Her words read as fresh as though written yesterday.

I stationed Aldrich's book on the round glass table on which I often write. If the table were a clockface, she sat at one o'clock, at first glance. It was as though I were writing her back, as her unnamed pen pal. It seemed a way to overcome the doubt that accompanies writing. A letter to begin a story. A way in. A device reinforced by author John McPhee in his book *Draft No. 4.*

"Dear Mother," he begins. "A bear can run nose-to-nose with Secretariat."

Then you snip off the salutation and tell the bear story.

"Dear Grandfather," I began, that winter of 2017, when I started drafting experimental chapters to the ghost of my grandfather, drawing upon primary source material: his own letters. I had found a thousand of them entombed intact in his basement storage room. He had been trained to keep records in his role as personal secretary for banker and horse breeder Major August Belmont II.

Acting on Major Belmont's orders, Grandfather had sold the great racehorse Man o' War as a yearling at Saratoga in August of 1918. I stumbled onto his voluminous correspondence from that era. His letters felt epic to me, something to be shared with an audience of horse fans, of history buffs. They read as if written yesterday, addressed not only to giants of the Turf such as Belmont, but to other patrons in the Golden Age of Horse Racing. Wall Street wizards. Gilded Age industrialists. Hollywood crooners assembling stables of racehorses. Most poignant, though, were letters to his three sons away in World War II.

Whenever I touched his swirling signature on a letter, a former world swam upstream to mine. All Grandfather needed to tell his story was a ghostwriter, a latter-day diarist, a wannabe biographer. Whether he chose me or I chose him, away we went together, his letters, my distillations, through thirty-eight monthly installments for the leading trade periodical in the horse business, *BloodHorse*.

Beginning the first month of 2018, the "Letters from Rockland Farm" column told how the horse business of Grandfather's era impacted the horse business of my day, which is a battle fought on many fronts: against a declining annual foal crop, against pressure from land development, against public indifference or indignation to the sport of horse racing, and, more often than necessary, against ourselves.

I wrote the *BloodHorse* series under the guise of "Rockland" because that was the name of this farm when Grandfather bought it in 1933. For the title of this book, citing Grandfather as precedent, I have changed the name of the Rockland series to more precisely read "Letters from Country Life."

A word on form. Letters and excerpts are set off by spacing and typeface. I have reconstructed Rockland chapters to flow into longer pieces, in chronological order—most of the time. The interval between the Rockland conclusion in 2021 and the publication of this book in 2024 allowed me to expand into materials previously unpublished in the magazine version. Here I cite another author and book I admire: Barbara Tuchman's *The Guns of August*. In her Author's Note, she writes:

> I have tried to avoid spontaneous attribution or the "he must have" style of historical writing: "As he watched the coastline of France disappear, Napolean must have thought back over the long. . . ."
>
> States of mind, public or private, have documentary support.

I too enjoy the certainty of documentary support, as in, Grandfather and his family boarded the steamship *Chateau Lafite* in 1888 at the French port of Bordeaux to come to America. But in a takeoff of Tuchman, I offer this lone spontaneous attribution:

> As he watched the coastline of France disappear, Grandfather could not imagine that a grandson he would never meet would one day discover the letters he would someday write.

As I write this, artificial intelligence chatbots are bringing grandfathers back to life everywhere. Feed enough letters into algorithms, you'll hear your questions answered by ancestors. For the sake of all your descendants, now and in the ages to come:

August 2024
Dear Grandfather,
I hope I got your story right.

Josh Pons
Country Life Farm

The stairs from the attic.

Part 1

ONE SHORT REMOVE

It's Christmas morning. I'm alone in the attic. The entire top floor of an elegant old farmhouse. Below the blown-glass windows roll the one hundred acres of Maryland's oldest Thoroughbred horse farm. Holidays trigger reflection. How did I get here? Where did I come from? I stare at the pitched angle of the steep eaves. White plaster walls meet honey-colored closets. Imagination takes over. I sense spirits pressing against the spring-loaded latches of the warped tongue-and-groove doors. When I touch the latches, it is as though I've broken the surface tension, and the doors spill open. Sunlight falls onto a shelf. A sky-blue envelope spools out like a proclamation. I read the first line out loud, a legal recital, a formal vow:

TO HAVE AND TO HOLD

It is the 1933 deed to Rockland Farm.

All that certain tract containing
one hundred one and four-tenths acres.

My grandfather, Adolphe Pons, was three months shy of his fiftieth birthday when he bought Rockland Farm in 1933 and renamed it Country Life Farm. Not quite a century ago but bearing down on it. He had served for twenty-five years as personal secretary to New York banker August Belmont II, the most important figure in American horse racing. As a young clerk in the Belmont & Co. Bank, Grandfather was schooled in the importance of keeping accurate records. He filed copies of everything: terse telegrams, lovely letters, formal photographs—a record of American life spanning the first half of the twentieth century.

On the same shelf as the Rockland deed, the front page of the Harford County weekly newspaper *The Aegis and Harford Gazette*:

Dateline: Friday, Dec. 28, 1951

ADOLPHE A. PONS, SR.
DIES TUESDAY, CHRISTMAS DAY
AT COUNTRY LIFE FARM

One of the nation's foremost authorities on Thoroughbred horses . . . 68 years old . . . in failing health for several months . . . sold the great Discovery to Alfred Gwynne Vanderbilt . . . active, genial, and a great lover of people and home life . . . liked by young and old alike.

Adolphe Pons before World War II.

Adolphe A. Pons, Sr. Dies Tuesday At Country Life Farm

Mr. Adolphe Adrian Pons, 68, long recognized as one of the nation's foremost authorities on blood-lines of thoroughbred horses, died on Tuesday night at Country Life Farm, near Bel Air. He had been in failing health for several months.

A native of France, Mr. Pons came to this country at the age of five years. For 24 years he was business agent for the late August Belmont, who had very extensive racing interests, and during that period became well acquainted with prominent horsemen throughout the United States.

On numerous occasions Mr. Pons negotiated thoroughbred deals running into fabulous sums. Among other transactions he handled the dispersal of Belmont Nursery Stud, gross proceeds from which amounted to more than $1,000,000. Big name horses were constantly under his care, and nothing gave him more pleasure than to bring buyer and seller together in a transaction which proved mutually beneficial. For instance, he sold the great Discovery to Alfred Gwynn Vanderbilt, and made many other notable sales in this and foreign countries.

Came To Harford In 1934

Mr. Pons purchased Country Life Farm, a short distance from Bel Air, in 1934 and since that time has bred many valuable horses on the property, in addition to boarding top broodmares belonging to others.

He was promptly recognized as a great addition to Maryland horse breeding interests and eventually became Vice-President and a Director of the Maryland Horse Breeders Association. He has also been a director of the Harford County Fair Association since its reorganization under the present management.

By many horsemen, Mr. Pons will best be remembered as an authority on bloodlines, having ac-

(Continued on page 8, col. 1)

Adolphe Pons obituary.

Above his obituary, accounts of true tragedies. Teens in a deadly car crash. A young father found wedged between boulders in the Gunpowder River. My mind jumps to everyday risks on a farm. Fell out of a hayloft. Kicked by a horse. Pinned under a tractor.

Thankfully, that wasn't you, Grandfather. You didn't die in a farming accident, but of a blood clot broken free from a frail heart. You died on the farm you bought two decades earlier for your family to grow up on, and which they have always loved. You died in the room below this attic, at 8:30 on a distant Christmas night. But you left the path for me to find you—your signature on documents, your thoughts in letters. And while most books about someone's life end in their death, this book picks up where death left off. Standing before the long-closed closet doors, I sense a pleasant madness come over me. I am about to begin a very long conversation with an empty room, but I am not crazy. I am simply acting out the words of a sign I once saw carved in stone above the door to a college library:

SPEAK
TO THE PAST
AND IT
SHALL TEACH THEE

STALL OF FAME

Adolphe (pronounced with a soft *a*, as in apple) Adrian Pons. The only one of my four grandparents I never met. Born in France in 1883. Died in this house in 1951. I was born three years later. Most of what I knew of him came from a dog-eared clipping from the *Daily Racing Form*. The headline:

Noted Turfman Dies

Discoveries in the attic enticed me to explore a basement storeroom, hasp lock invitingly unlocked. I knew he had kept records in wooden filing cabinets, but I had never researched their contents. Brittle cardboard boxes obstructed my entrance. I put my shoulder into the door and pushed hard enough to reach in for the light switch. An overhead bulb flooded the room in a faint yellow. Sense of something vintage in that light. I had pushed through to the past.

On a chair with the canework seat half missing, I sat and read. Grandfather came alive in his own words, in what archivists refer to as "primary source material." Letters, as opposed to newspapers. First-hand accounts in longhand, or typewritten. Contemporaneous. In the moment.

Grandfather's letters had been safekept for a century in a room so out of the way no one ever needed the space. No one ever culled the contents. No periodic purging. No pirating. The oldest documents—undisturbed for one hundred years.

The room is the size of a yearling's stall: ten feet by ten feet. Six panel wooden door. A raised oak floor to keep contents dry from any bursting basement pipes. Inside, letters from the Golden Age of Horse Racing, the years before and after Man o' War—the Horse of the Century bred by Belmont in 1917.

First Easter at Country Life, 1934. Left to right: Aunt Peggy, Auntie Kas, Grandmother ("Nana": Mrs. Adolphe Pons) in white dress on wicker chair.

I begin ferrying boxes of archival papers up the forty-two steps to the attic, where sheets of plywood on sawhorses serve as examining tables. I arrange a rough chronology of curled photos of Easters and birthdays, of studio portraits, of faded brown images of horse people from racing publications. In every photo I find of him, Grandfather appears lost in concentration. Restless intensity in his eyes. Preoccupied.

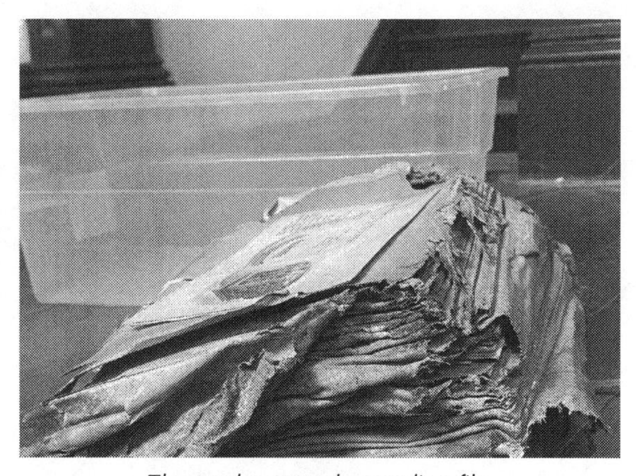

The smoke-scarred accordion file.

Contents of a smoke-stained, legal-sized accordion folder dated 1901 begin to tell his story. Early biographical material of young Adolphe, age eighteen, errand boy in his first year of employment in the Belmont bank. From the file falls a letter on elegant turn-of-the-century stationery:

S. Klaber & Co.
Art Workers in Marble

In 1901, Grandfather's father Flour (pronounced "fleur," as in fleur-de-lis), a French-born cook employed in the Belmont households, dies at forty-seven years old. Funeral arrangements are in the hands of teenage Adolphe, the eldest of three children.

A rare relic, this smoky file. Only a few charred documents made it out alive from the devasting 1912 fire in the Equitable Life Assurance Company building in downtown Manhattan, home to Belmont's bank office. I gingerly finger water-damaged papers streaked with blue ink that washed out into faint brushstrokes, lettering barely discernible, the file compressed shut for a century inside the thick accordion folds.

Lost to the blazes were the Belmont family's Nursery Stud records from 1867 through 1911. A treasure of horse history. The great racemare Beldame's 1904 championship campaign, when she was named Horse of

Fair Play with Hall of Fame jockey Joe Notter.

the Year. The career of Man o' War's sire Fair Play—his historic 1908 battles against undefeated champion Colin. Notes on breeding decisions that produced Man o' War's dam Mahubah, a foal of 1910. Irreplaceable equine archives of the Belmont empire perished in the fire.

The accordion file is a delicate matter. I coax it apart. Pages pressed by time reveal eureka moments, such as the Klaber letter. A year out of high school, Grandfather is asking Mr. Klaber to please leave three empty spaces following Flour's name on the family headstone. What fate does he anticipate as he pencil-sketches a grid of four gravesites? Perhaps just the fatalistic reality of life in that age of tuberculosis, of unchecked pandemics. He writes an inscription in French for Mr. Klaber to chisel in marble:

A La Memoire
de
Flour A. Pons
Décédé le 17 Janvier 1901
A L'Age de 47 Ans.

Adolphe is the man of the house now. Dreams of college set aside. Maybe he takes clerical courses in the Teacher's College at Columbia (still a college then, not a university until 1912). I recall proud family lore that Grandfather had graduated from Columbia, but when I visit the admissions office to confirm this anecdote, they can find no record of him.

"Records from back then are incomplete. So many immigrants had to learn the language, learn the skills necessary to build this great city of New York. Many came through here, but we have no record of your grandfather."

And I have no informal nickname for him. He wasn't Gandy Pops. He wasn't Granddaddy. He was always simply identified to me as "your grandfather."

My grandfather was born in 1883 in the town of Gignac near Montpellier, forty miles from the Mediterranean Sea in the south of France. The family moved to the Twelfth Arrondissement in Paris, along the river Seine, southeast of Notre Dame Cathedral. His father Flour was trained as a chef, an honored occupation in France, world-famous for its cuisine.

According to the American Family Immigration History Center at Ellis Island, Flour arrived *en famille* in New York Harbor on July 2, 1894, aboard the *La Normandie.* It was Flour's second trip to America, having first come over in 1887 as a chef for the Robert Garrett family in Baltimore.

The *La Normandie*'s port of departure was Le Havre, on the English Channel. From the passenger manifest:

```
Pons  Flour, age 40
      Elisa, 35
      Adolphe, 12 (Author's note: He was actually 10.)
      Etienne, 10
      Marie, 8
```

Flour will become a naturalized American citizen, a status extended to his French-born wife and their three French-born children. For ease in assimilation, immigrants would Americanize their names. Flour begins signing his name F. Adrien Pons. Elisa becomes Elizabeth. Grandfather's middle name, Adrien, is soon spelled with an *a*, more masculine than the French *e*.

Flour has been brought over from Paris to become chef for the Belmont family, who entertain in the lavish style of the Gilded Age. He prepares elaborate dinners at Belmont's mansion on Fifth Avenue, at Belmont's Nursery Stud estate on Long Island near Babylon (just inland from today's Jones Beach), and at Belmont's BytheSea, the family's summer home in Rhode Island's famed resort town of Newport, off whose waters was contested the first *America*'s Cup yacht races.

Among Grandfather's records in the burnt accordion file is Flour's deed for their house at 353 Broadway, Newport's main street, at the intersection of Fowler Avenue. On a vacation visit to Newport, I stopped outside my *great*-grandfather's former home, imagining ancestors I never knew, seaside summers in the late 1800s, Narragansett Bay a block away. Across Fowler Avenue is the Memorial Funeral Home. A bit spooked by so many spirits lingering about the neighborhood, I walked uphill to Bellevue—the boulevard of opulent mansions overlooking cliffs that drop to the sea. (BytheSea was torn down in the 1940s.)

Flour will only live seven years in his adopted country before he dies of pneumonia in 1901. He is one of 1,750,000 souls buried in Calvary Cemetery, on a hill in Queens, overlooking the East River. For the family record, he lies interred in Section 16, Range 11, Plot H, Grave 3. When I see a photo online of the cemetery, I am struck by how the foreground of slender vertical obelisks and monuments mirrors the backdrop of Manhattan skyscrapers, as if foretelling the shape of the city to come. I vow to someday visit Plot H, hopefully not in a box.

THE BELMONT BOYS

Inside the main house at Country Life, it's a war zone. Wide swaths of plaster punched away. Wooden lathing exposed. Furniture, desks pushed up against walls. Dust clings to enormous plastic sheeting draped down stairwells. The see-through sheets billow in drafts from fireplace openings. Blackened porcelain insulators show through walls where electricians have sawed holes. The ancient knob-and-tube wiring of Thomas Edison's era is being abandoned, replaced with the white flexible plastic of Romex wiring. Grandfather's spirit seems pleased. Anything to lessen the chance of fire.

I climb through the protective plastic curtains, reach the attic, resume my research. The nine-story Equitable Life Assurance building is the first in the world to have passenger elevators. The night of the 1912 fire, the thermometer reads six degrees. A shivering nightwatchman flicks a match. That's all it takes. Spray from fire hoses sculpts layers of ice onto the sidewalks. Trapped firemen leap to their deaths. Two months pass. Business resumes. Grandfather writes:

March 7th, 1912
Dear Mr. Murphy:

I have not received any bill itemized. It may have been destroyed in the Equitable fire or mislaid during the confusion of moving.

Knob-and-tube wiring.

So much wood in building materials; fuel for so many fires. The *New York Times* reports arsons of training barns at New York racetracks. Grandfather orders fire extinguishers sent to the barn of Belmont's trainer, Sam Hildreth. A photograph from that era shows Grandfather standing between trainer Louie Feustel and jockey Joe Notter. Feustel blows cigar smoke at Grandfather as Notter's cigar burns to a nub in his fingers. How many smoldering cigars were flicked into shedrows?

Photographer C. C. Cook used the dry-plate negative process to take this picture. The glass plates are in safekeeping at the Keeneland Library in Lexington, Kentucky. Library Directors Becky Ryder and Roda Ferraro give me a lesson in archive etiquette. Be mindful of the age of artifacts. Use a micro-spatula to gently open letters.

Ryder and Ferraro search for photos of Grandfather. This triggers a deep dive into all things Belmont. Copies of century-old clippings begin arriving from the Keeneland Library. So much of racing's history traces to the Belmont family. The race named the Belmont Stakes and the racetrack named Belmont Park honor August Belmont I, president of the American Jockey Club from 1866 to 1886. The Jockey Club, as we know it today, was founded in 1894; August Belmont II presided over it from 1896 until his death in 1924. Here in the attic, records of father and son reside inside wire-reinforced Gaylord archival storage boxes. I open the files to find a one-hundred-year-old pamphlet:

Feustel, Pons, and Notter.

HISTORY OF THE BELMONT STAKES
The Oldest Classic for Three-Year-Olds
in the United States

By W. S. Vosburgh

Inaugurated at Jerome Park in 1867
To Be Run at Belmont Park, June 10, 1922
Value $50,000

Writes the author Walter S. Vosburgh:

> Even as a child I recognized its importance, and regard "Belmont Day" with a reverence not unlike Christmas or Independence Day.

I set out on a search for the first August Belmont. He lived from 1813 to 1890. In Victorian-era photographs, he seems lifeless, like a wax figure. The narrative that accompanied his entry into the National Museum of Racing and Hall of Fame in 2019 is helpful, but Belmont is a tough subject to resuscitate. In every photo, he's inscrutable. Bill Leggett of *Sports Illustrated*, though, breathed life into the frozen figure simply by adding context.

> Although little is known now about the man for whom Belmont Park is named, he saved American racing.

August Belmont I portrait and family album.

By adopting England's Rules of Racing, and then enforcing them, Belmont indeed saved the young sport of horse racing in America. I find an elegant studio album of Belmont family photos. It was once adorned with filigreed metalwork tapped into a wooden cover that opened with hinges and latches. Intricate. Old World. But the metal closures have rusted to dust, and the ornate album falls apart in my hands. Ghost-written in black ink on the first photo: Hon. August Belmont. He earned the "Honorable" by serving as America's emissary to The Hague in the Netherlands in the mid-1850s. In the first photo of the family album, I see the camera's catch-light caught in the Hon. August Belmont's eyes, and I feel honored to be introduced to him. Onto a sawhorse table I heft a 1912 collection of works by sculptor John Quincy Adams Ward. The title of the book is *An Appreciation*. Out falls this handwritten note:

> One day this sculptor received a visit from a gentleman halting a little in his step, who wished a bronze of his father-in-law, Commodore Matthew C. Perry, he who opened the Philippines to the world. This request from August Belmont was my first commission.

Ward's sculpture of Belmont looks so static to me. This is not the Belmont I'm learning about. My Belmont never stopped moving, despite his being lame for life after a duel in 1841, when he took a bullet to the hip, luckily not the heart. He drove four-in-hand coaches, wildly at times. He persuaded the Rothschild banks in Europe to back the Union in the Civil War. He maintained herd books for bulls and horses at the Nursery, never missed the races at Saratoga, danced all night at masquerade balls in his Fifth Avenue mansion, strolled along Cliff Walk beneath the awnings of BytheSea. While judging a coaching-stallion competition at Madison Square Garden in the fall of 1890, he took ill, and died soon thereafter of pneumonia. He seems miscast in Ward's bronze statue—brooding, ponderous—when in fact he whirled through a fascinating life. Except for a few days in bed after being wounded in the duel, he seems never to have been immobile.

TOP HAT AND GREATCOAT

Who wouldn't marvel at a 130-year-old book as perfect as the day it was printed?

NURSERY STUD SALE
1891

The catalog for the dispersal of August Belmont I's Thoroughbred horses opens with a photogravure: an etching of him in a top hat and a greatcoat. A walking stick protrudes from his fur-cuffed sleeve. He limped from the age of twenty-five. The duel took place in a field near Elkton, Maryland, twenty miles from where I sit typing. In storybook style, he was defending a woman's honor, that of Caroline Perry, daughter of Commodore Perry.

Chance reigned. Had the bullet been fatal, no August Belmont II, no need for chef Flour Pons, or for the chef's son Adolphe. No Man o' War. No Country Life. The subject material of this book unfolds simply because Belmont did not die in a duel in 1841. The ancient autocrat is alive and well, right here in this attic, poking his walking stick at me, exhorting: "Make sure to get your facts right."

RISING SON

Of the second August Belmont, attic archives overflow. Carbons of his letters lift and snap in the breeze of a floor fan. A distant Decoration Day is the subject of a May 1916 memo from Belmont, as president of the Westchester Racing Association, operator of Belmont Park. Prominent sportsman Harry Payne Whitney has asked Belmont to allow a steeplechase race on the popular holiday, a big betting day. Belmont is reluctant:

> Dear Harry,
> Our races do not begin until May 25th. The racing in Maryland stops on May 17th . . . amateur meetings could be held between those two dates.

Gamblers consider it a sucker's game to wager on steeplechases, where horses tumble over fences, unseat riders, disqualify themselves. As a favor to Whitney, though, Belmont cards a jumping race, but gets in the last word:

> When there is an attendance of 30,000 to 40,000, I remind you that the necessity of revenue is vital.

The Golden Age of Horse Racing. How about that? Forty thousand fans, routinely. The floor fan snaps another letter to attention. Arnold

Rothstein, who will stand trial in 1921 for fixing the 1919 World Series, is seeking a meeting with Belmont.

August 17, 1920

My dear Mr. Belmont:
The Brook Clubs restaurant is opened and those who are interested in racing tell me it adds greatly to the attraction of Saratoga, and a matter of importance has arisen which I should like to lay before you.

With respect,
Arnold Rothstein

Rothstein is the model for Meyer Wolfsheim in F. Scott Fitzgerald's classic *The Great Gatsby*. I can almost smell bootlegged rum as I run my fingers over Rothstein's signature, so strong is the scent I'm following, so powerful are these primary sources from the past.

HORSES ON THE HIGH SEAS

In Grandfather's basement storage room, a pair of white seahorses are painted on brown plaster. Three feet tall, they appear buoyant, as though

Basement seahorses.

walking on water, as though weightless. They face each other, mythical mirror images. Long-nosed horse heads on curled tails. Manes straight up on curved necks. Silent sentries since God knows when. From the earliest days of this old house, for all I know.

Each time I ferry files from basement to attic, I pause at the incredible lightness of the seahorses—spirit descendants of early man's paintings of horses on walls in the Lascaux Caves of Grandfather's France. On shelves when I reach high, I am eye-to-eye with the seahorses.

"Why are you going to all this trouble?" they seem to ask, gently mocking me.

Good question. As if in reply, a fresh treasure tumbles out of the last box under the seahorses' gaze. A first edition *Blooded Horses of Colonial Days*, by Francis Barnum Culver. Published in Baltimore in 1922. Introduced with an ancient horsey poem by Virgil:

The rules of war to know;
T'obey the rider,
and to dare the foe.

The essence of horse racing: A dare to see who owns the fastest horse, and a foe to take the bet. I flip to page eighty, puzzle over a sort of condition book from 1745: At a three-day fair in "Baltimore Town," a race "will be run for any Horse, Mare, or Gelding; three heats, to carry 125 pounds weight."

Does this race presage the Preakness? Did it include a racing steward? Apparently so: "All Disputes that may arise, to be determined by Charles Ridgley."

Follow this thread with me. Grandfather is the right-hand man for Belmont, the chairman of The Jockey Club, supreme arbiter of racing disputes. Belmont's *Racing Manuals* are bound in black leather, somber as church missals. A crusader for clean racing, Belmont carries considerable sway in the legislative halls of Albany, but not enough to offset the anti-gambling Progressive movement. In 1908, New York passes the Hart-Agnew Law, carrying a killer clause for racetrack owners: They are subject to arrest for *any* gambling conducted on their track premises. By 1911, all New York tracks have shut down. Gravesend and Sheepshead Bay never reopen. Wealthiest owners expatriate their horses. Belmont's Kentucky-bred Tracery boards a steamship for Europe. In 1912, Tracery made the first start of his career in the most famous race in the world, the Epsom Derby. He finished third, then he won the classic St. Leger Stakes. He was leading

Rules of Racing manuals in somber black covers.

in the Ascot Gold Cup when a pistol-brandishing suffragette jumped into the homestretch and toppled him. As World War I begins, so too does the exodus of the best blooded horses of England, France, and Ireland. They are bound for New York, where racing has resumed. Tides of war have turned the steamships around.

KANE CAN EXPLAIN

Voluminous correspondence between Grandfather, manager of the business of Belmont's horses, and Elizabeth Kane, manager of the actual four-legged, living, breathing horses at Belmont's Nursery Stud near Lexington, Kentucky.

Kane's letters require patient transcription. Her handwriting is hasty, often illegible. I decipher one word at a time, relying on context, convinced that these are the lost letters of the Willa Cather of horsewomen, a pioneering female in a world of horsemen. Compulsive. Cathartic. Quick to compliment, to criticize. Sometimes three letters in one week to Grandfather. Often four pages long.

"It is almost impossible to read my handwriting," she apologizes in a rare typewritten letter.

The ink in her pen can't keep pace. Words fade until she fetches a fresh inkwell. Readers crack her code: *O*s aren't circular but slanted; *T*s aren't crossed immediately but slashed a moment later as though suddenly remembered; *L*s in lowercase contain no loop. She races through everyday problems in letters to Grandfather eight hundred miles away in Belmont's Wall Street office. The two managers are co-dependents. She is cryptic:

> I'm glad we didn't sell Fair Play.
> We need new fencing.
> I'm saving up for a machine. (Author's note: What she calls an automobile.)
> I can wait on electricity.

She takes over management of the Nursery upon the death of her husband, Edward Kane, in spring 1917. That summer, when she forwards farm bills to New York for payment by Grandfather as Belmont's fiscal agent, she includes photos of eleven foals. She is battling a strangles outbreak on the farm. Equine distemper. Graphic evidence is one photo in particular: skilled fingers, likely Kane's, steady a sick foal's head—eyes swollen shut, lymph glands battling infection, throat latch oozing with abscesses. Mind you: This is ten years before the discovery of penicillin.

A 1917 foal afflicted with equine distemper.

July 6, 1917

I hope they will soon pick up for they are a sorry lot. Mr. Pons, I would thank you for any advice or any criticisms.

Yours very truly,
Elizabeth Kane

The sick baby in the photo is not Man o' War, but it's a fellow member of his foal crop of 1917, and a truism in this game is that the best horses have the worst luck. How differently the history of horse racing would read if, as a mere foal, Man o' War had succumbed to strangles.

To my practiced eye, Kane's near-terrible penmanship is now near-readable. Her cursive strokes swim wildly over the page, penned in haste by a busy woman working hard on the frontlines of the horse business.

Frontlines of another kind occupy Kane's mind in May of 1918. American involvement in the Great War is escalating. She worries about her son Kent—"as he is wild to go to France." Stationed at Camp Zachary Taylor in Louisville, Kent is a knowledgeable young horseman surrounded by thousands of packhorses bound for New York harbor, where the horses will be loaded on ships bound for France to resupply cavalries, pull caissons, get gassed on the Western Front. Historians estimate that ten million horses died in World War I.

At Camp Zachary Taylor, soldiers of the American Expeditionary Forces are battling the deadly Spanish flu epidemic of 1918. Kane sends this dispatch to Grandfather during Kentucky Derby week:

Being in the Hospital Corps, he has to go through the wards where they are dying with all kinds of disease which makes it more dangerous than the Germans. I am going to see Kent. . . . I will be in Louisville at the Watterson Hotel from Sat-noon until Mon-noon . . . wire me there.

Major Belmont, at sixty-four years old, is in Paris, four thousand miles from Lexington, calling on Rothschild banking clients to help finance the Allied effort. Kane fears for the Major, and for the lives of her gifted horsemen sons Alfred and Kent, and for the health of her trusted confidant, Grandfather. Lengthy passages in her letters say nothing of horses, but much about life during wartime.

THE MAJOR'S ORDERS

America entered World War I on April 6, 1917, three years after it began. On April 10, four days into the war, Grandfather writes to family members in France:

> We will act so quick the Germans will be finished in three months. If the Americans open an unlimited credit to the Allies, we will see the end of this war before America sends troops over.

Of course, he's wrong. The troops we send over include Major Belmont, who is the oldest commissioned officer in World War I. His departure has left Grandfather in charge.

"Sell my horses," Major Belmont orders him. "We must help the war effort."

Reason enough, but another impulse is prodding the Major: promissory notes for the construction loans of the Cape Cod Canal, an ambitious project fraught with engineering issues. Steam shovels strike rock lurking below surface sand. Tides swing erratically. Opened to ship traffic in 1914, the canal may have been the first American victim of the war. German U-boats off the Atlantic Coast torpedo merchant vessels, shell tugboats. Belmont's business plan for the canal relies on tolls. Of course, those receipts plummet. With no end in sight in the war that was supposed to end all wars, horsemen are not buying the most liquid of Belmont's assets:

> Woodburn Farm, Spring Station, Ky. June 12, 1917
>
> To: Mr. Adolphe Pons
>
> Dear Sir:
>
> Mr. Kenneth Alexander has left for France to join the Ambulance Corps, and he is not in the market for any horses now.
>
> Very truly yours,
> A.J.A. Alexander

Claiborne Farm, Paris, Ky, July 10, 1917.

To: Adolphe Pons Esq.
Racing Sec'y to Mr. August Belmont

Dear Sir,
I appreciate Mr. Belmont's offer to sell Trap Rock, but I cannot now buy him.

Sincerely yours,
A.B. Hancock

Nevertheless, Belmont is appreciative of Grandfather's efforts, even though futile.

Paris, December 1, 1917

Adolphe Pons,
I am very much pleased with your attention to my affairs.

Maybe selling Man o' War was Belmont's way to help the war effort? Makes for a patriotic press release. The shame of it is that Man o' War is sold at Saratoga in 1918 a mere three months before the end of the endless war. The best horse any breeder ever bred, sold away.

LAST POST

Grandfather turns thirty-five the day the Great War ends. The centennial anniversary of Armistice Day occurs on Grandfather's 135th birthday. His US War Department draft card bears the postmark:

Brooklyn N.Y.
NOV 9
12PM 1918

With two-day delivery, Grandfather would have received his Selective Service card on November 11, his birthday, the morning the war ends, church bells ringing out across the world. A lone bugler in the fields of France sounds "Last Post," eerie and evocative, charged with the memory of men who died in the war that ended on the eleventh hour of the eleventh day of the eleventh month of 1918. I slip silently out of the garret, spooked by my morning finds, by my runaway imagination. All those elevens. Two of my own to add to the collection: 11:11 a.m., June 27, 1954. So reads my birth certificate.

On his 135th birthday, Grandfather walks beside me along Winters Run, the sound of rushing water loud and steady and soothing. Paths on the forest floor echo with the footfalls of time. First the wildlife—elk and deer, brown and black bears—padding past, opening the way. Then the Native Americans, the roaming Susquehannocks, hunting those elk, pausing to carve pictographs of game animals on Susquehanna River cliff-rock up the Chesapeake Bay. Then the King of England's lumberjacks in search of straight trees for ship masts, floating timbers down Winters Run to the Chesapeake Bay bound for the British Navy. Then grist millers grinding wheat on water-powered wheels, soon followed by cattle farmers, their barbed wire still evident, still stiletto sharp despite having grown into the trunks of beech trees. And finally, a horse farmer, a breeder of fine Thoroughbreds, settling on this well-watered land. That's you, Grandfather.

Here is my absolute favorite photograph of you. In blue ink in the white margins above and below the photo, the words *Winters Run* and the year *1933*. You are standing alone on the riverbank below the graceful arch of the Route 1 bridge over the rapids. You are dressed as though you just stepped off the train. You never paused long anywhere, but in this picture, you are savoring the peace of your new farm.

Grandfather standing at Winters Run

"Thank you for the chance to live here," I say out loud. I am a grandson he never saw, but I feel as though he is seeing me now when I imagine him say:

"None of us are here long. Don't take a moment for granted."

Man o' War as a foal.

Nursery Stud, 1917. Foal Crop. Star-and-snip, Man o' War is third foal in photo.

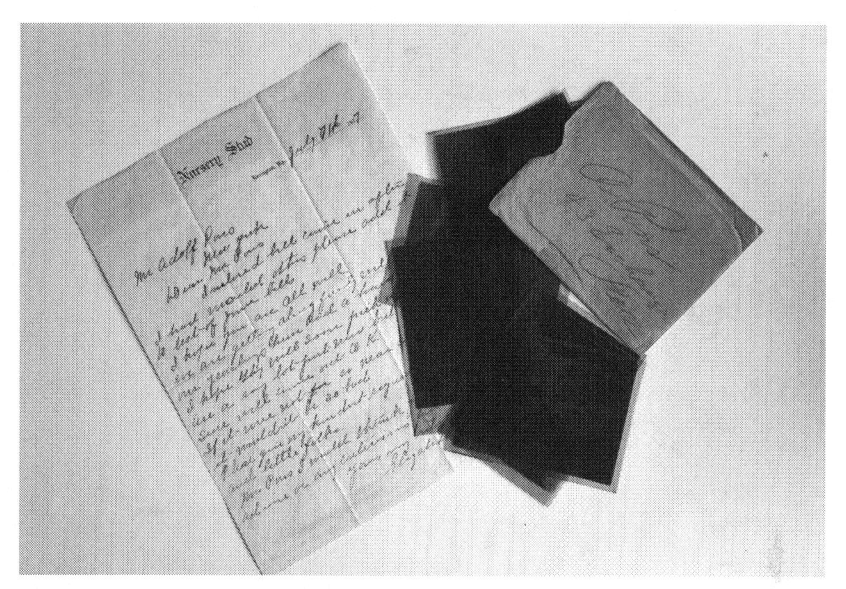

Elizabeth Kane's letter with the Man o' War negatives.

Back in the attic, I stare at a thick cardboard box I'm sure I've never seen: The Oxford Sliding Drawer Storage File. Steel handles are fitted with fat washers. This is a formidable file box. Buried in this cardboard coffin: a graveyard of letters. I have stumbled upon the mother lode of Grandfather's Nursery Stud correspondence.

July 7, 1917. A letter from Kane. Her envelope contains four faded photographs and eleven negatives. I hold one of the negatives to the light, discern a leggy foal with unusual markings—wide white star connected to a thin stripe that fades out then reappears even thinner. The foal is not wearing a halter. Nothing obstructs my view of his face as he grazes beside his dam. Same big foal—third from left in another negative—pushing into position at a wooden creep feeder. No one has seen these photos since they were filed away in 1917, and here I am, staring into the face of Man o' War.

DISPATCHES

When a horse breeder names a yearling, it is a signal of intent to race, not to sell. Despite his intent, Belmont will not race the yearling his wife has named Man o' War. In August of 1918, twenty-four Nursery Stud yearlings, many named by Mrs. Belmont for military terms, arrive at the Saratoga sales grounds after an arduous forty-three-hour train ride from Kentucky. Grandfather reports to Major Belmont:

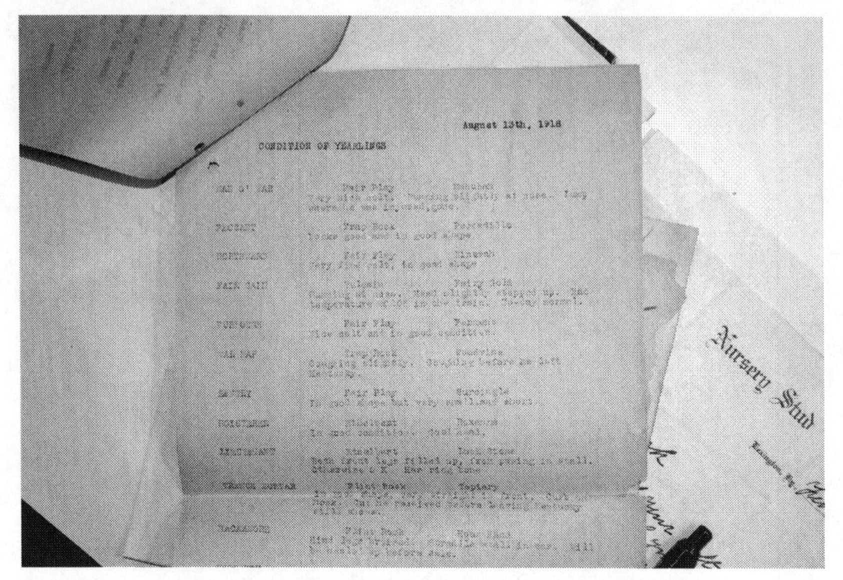

Freshly discovered 1918 report by Grandfather to Belmont.

August 13th, 1918

MEMO. SARATOGA

YEARLINGS - The yearlings arrived on Sunday morning about eight o'clock. They were loaded at Greendale about 1 o'clock Friday afternoon, left at 3 o'clock, remained in station at Cincinnati 2 hours, and held in yards at Cleveland for nearly 5 hours.

The cars they shipped in were miserable ones, some of the oldest horse cars, now used for shipping cattle unstalled.

Willie (the groom) complained to the Agent in Lexington about these cars and told the Agent that he understood the three-door steel car and a two-door palace horse car, very comfortable, which the Agent gave to Mr. Headley, were intended for our use.

The Agent told him very freshly that he better take the two wooden cars or he would get none.

Luckily, the horses stood the trip fairly well.

Adolphe Pons

By mere historic whim, the *very first yearling* among the twenty-four on Grandfather's dispatch to Belmont is:

MAN O' WAR
Fair Play—Mahubah
Very nice colt. Running slightly at nose. Lump where he was injured, gone.

A sampling of Grandfather's other examinations:

GUN MUZZLE
Tracery—Gallows Hill
In good shape but slightly running at nose. Cut on left hind leg.

TRENCH MORTAR
Flint Rock—Topiary
Very straight in front. Curb on hock. Cut he received before leaving Kentucky still shows.

LIEUTENANT
Ethelbert—Luck Stone
Both front legs filled up, from pawing in stall. Otherwise, O. K. Has ring bone.

SENTRY
Fair Play—Surcingle
In good shape but very small and short.

TOURNIQUET
Fair Play—Togger
A big, nice filly. Should sell well.

WAR MAP
Trap Rock—Woodvine
Coughing slightly. Coughing before he left Kentucky.

Grandfather identifies prospective buyers:

Mr. Walter J. Salmon specially liked the Mahubah, Fairy Gold, and Ferment colts. I overheard him say later to Mr. Hancock he would try and buy the Mahubah colt at any price.

Mr. Wayland, Phil Chinn, and Mrs. Walsh also looked at them. I also spoke to Mr. Butler, Mr. Riddle, and Mr. Jeffords.

Consider this: Belmont's broodmare band is exquisite, the best in the business. Still, Grandfather singles out four poor yearlings from those grand mares.

> I am afraid that some will not sell very well and may get no bid: for instance, the Surcingle, Queen of Trent, Delusion, and Toucan.

Modern sales catalogs elaborate on an agent's Code of Conduct, on Conflicts of Interest. Fifty pages of legalese just to protect horse sellers and buyers. Not so in the old days. You were either trusted or you weren't. Grandfather discloses to Major Belmont that a buyer approached him with a scheme in mind—the old gamble to buy low but at a fixed price (before the sale) then turn around with hopes to sell high (through the sales ring), often with an enticing undisclosed kickback to the agent.

> George Smith offered me $20,000 for the whole lot and let the sale go on just the same. I refused the offer.

This example of his honesty makes me proud to be his grandson. The sale goes on as planned. Samuel D. Riddle, Jr. buys Man o' War for five thousand dollars. Later that summer, Major Belmont returns from the war. Mahubah's colt becomes Horse of the Century for someone else. Belmont dies in 1924. Four years later, the US government issues bonds to buy out the beleaguered Cape Cod Canal. Man o' War didn't race for Belmont. Life is messy.

MAN O' WAR STORIES

Books everywhere I look. Tomes fill tabletops: Colonel John Wall's two-volume *Thoroughbred Bloodlines: An Elementary Study* opens to a photograph of high-headed Man o' War, followed by a fold-out chart terracing his ancestors back to the 1724 birth of the Godolphin Arabian.

The six-part series *Racing in America, 1665–1979*. Bound in linen. Ragged-cut edges of vellum paper. Honor roll of incomparable authors: John Hervey, Walter Vosburgh, Robert Kelley, William Rudy. Vosburgh presented signed copies to members of The Jockey Club. Belmont's second wife, Eleanor, presented her late husband's copy to Grandfather, provenance authenticated by letters and books that add context. I dive into history.

After buying Man o' War as a yearling at Saratoga, Riddle sends the colt to his Glen Riddle Farm in Berlin, Maryland, four miles west of the beach resort of Ocean City. By March of 1919, Man o' War is breezing around the farm's state-of-the-art, one-mile training track. Grandfather writes to his boyhood pal Louie Feustel, Man o' War's trainer, that jockey Johnny Loftus might not be granted a license to ride this year. Loftus is the "first call" rider for the Riddle stable. Is Grandfather leaking privileged information? Major Belmont, back from the war, has resumed his duties as chairman of The Jockey Club. Certainly, Grandfather has inside information on issues. Feustel wastes no time replying.

March 9, 1919

Dear Pons:

Regarding Loftus, I am afraid he will not get it . . . as you ought to know a little about it. But if he is not going to be straight, we may be better off.

If he does not get his license, I have saved Mr. Riddle a lot of money, we are paying him $500.00 per month and expenses.

Sincerely yours,
Louis Feustel

March 20, 1919

Dear Louis:

Be on the lookout for a good jockey, as it looks practically sure that neither Loftus nor Lyke will be granted licenses this year.

Adolphe

Grandfather and Feustel are a year ahead of The Jockey Club's sentencing of Loftus. For the racing season of 1919, Loftus rides Man o' War in all ten of the two-year-old champion's races. A lone upset, though, to a horse named Upset in the Sanford Stakes, attracts suspicion of race-fixing. Fallout from the World Series scandal in October of 1919 lands on other professional sports. In the spring of 1920, without explanation, The Jockey Club denies Loftus a license. Feustel scrambles:

April 7, 1920
Glen Riddle Farm, Berlin, Md.

Dear Pons:

Man o' War is doing fine and expect to stay here until May 1st and then ship to Belmont Park and my first start will be in the Preakness if everything goes well.

We have no Jock now, all the best boys are engaged and everybody cannot ride Man o' War, but if it come to the worst I can ride him myself. Very truly yours,

Louis Feustel

Man o' War is spared the tiring train ride to Louisville and back for the May 8 Kentucky Derby. He makes his three-year-old debut in the May 15 Preakness Stakes. He will win all eleven races that year, under three different jockeys, but none under Loftus.

Lignin fibers in letters between Pons and Feustel have turned words brown, paper brittle. These are old letters written by young men, candidly autobiographical, their conversations captured in orderly folders undisturbed for one hundred years.

Not owning Man o' War gnaws away at Belmont. So does debt from the Cape Cod Canal. Belmont turns harsh in his treatment of his loyal, lifelong employees.

Feb 24th, 1920

My dear Mrs. Kane:

This is strictly confidential. Do not mention a word to anyone in Lexington, nor even hint about it when writing to the Major. I had a real falling out with him the other day and I am about through. You know a man can stand so much and no more, and the limit has been reached in my case. I have been with him 20 years in March and although I hate to leave here, I assure you I can locate elsewhere. I will resign. I am getting to be a nervous wreck.

Adolphe

Both Kane and Grandfather worry that Belmont, beset by creditors and suppressing regret over having sold Man o' War, will simply step away from the sport. Kane writes:

August 26, 1920

Mr. Pons, you are the only one I could possibly trust with this matter of great significance. I have heard it intimated several times the Major may sell out the entire Nursery stock and retire from breeding, and I have been reading about Mr. Riddle starting an establishment in Kentucky.

My son Alfred needs greater responsibilities. He is handicapped here. I cannot see a happy life for me without him. However, I do not want to stand in his light.

She also dreads the thought of anything happening to Grandfather:

I do not wonder that you are nervous with all of your responsibilities. We all need you very badly, so take care of yourself.

Kane herself is afflicted with rheumatoid arthritis, takes to her bed in two-week stretches, dictates letters to her daughter Frances who acts as stenographer, as typist. Her words confirm anecdotal accounts, to wit: Man o' War's owner Riddle is the apotheosis of stuffy Eastern Establishment. He visits the Nursery Stud looking for another champion, shopping for value, aware of Belmont's duress. Kane writes of her disdain for Riddle.

Nursery Stud
Lexington, Ky.
Oct. 18th, 1920

Dear Mr. Pons,

I can't tell you how much I regret that Man o' War doesn't belong to the Major. I do think Mr. Riddle is selfish. He never even congratulated us, and when he was at the Nursery, he never even gave the boys a tip.

Elizabeth Kane

She inveighs against the idea that Grandfather may leave his position as Belmont's secretary to oversee the expanding Xalapa Farm outside Paris, Kentucky, being developed by oilman Edward Simms. She slashes the word *Confidential* on this letter:

October 18th, 1920

Dear Mr. Pons,
I will drive you to the Simms estate. It is about as poorly managed an affair as one could imagine. The manager, Mr. Buckner, is a dub. He is a broken aristocrat and as self-conceited as one could be.

If Mr. Simms lives to be an old man, he will never see the work finished that has been started.

It is a lonesome out-of-the-way place, and I don't think you or Mrs. Pons would like it.

I know of no ambitious man who cares to work for them and therefore Mr. Simms can spend all the money he likes and will never make a success.

Elizabeth Kane

She's got Simms pegged, as she did Riddle. Simms is burning through a fortune. Pressured to pay bills in 1924, he puts his herds of Thoroughbreds onto train cars heading for New York's last horse auction of the year. When I search Grandfather's bound volumes of Fasig-Tipton catalogs from that era—stacks of black books four inches thick, edged in gold leaf—I find:

Dispersal of the Thoroughbreds from Xalapa Farm
December 10-11, 1924
E. J. Tranter, Auctioneer, assisted by S. C. Nuckols

Consider the sheer logistical challenge of transporting, by freight, all eight of Xalapa's stallions, ninety broodmares, forty-nine weanlings, twelve yearlings, and eleven horses in training—170 horses in total—from remote Kentucky to Squadron "A" Armory, at 94th Street and Madison Avenue in New York City, in winter no less. Kane marvels:

What do you think about Simms selling out? I hear he owes three million.

HORSE PATHS

Major Belmont envisioned a match race between England's 1923 Epsom Derby winner Papyrus and America's 1923 Kentucky Derby winner Zev. An international race. The best of theirs against the best of ours, decades before modern matches between Europeans and Americans in the Breed-

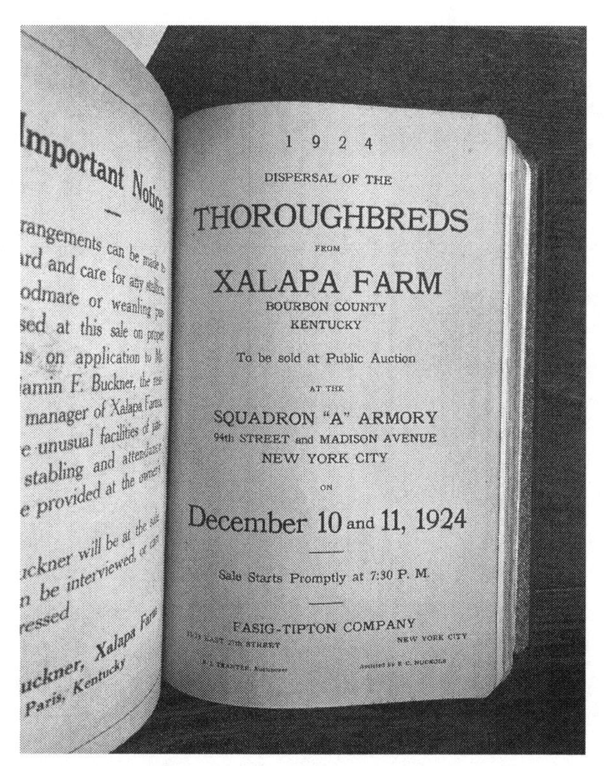
1 9 2 4

DISPERSAL OF THE

THOROUGHBREDS

FROM

XALAPA FARM

BOURBON COUNTY

KENTUCKY

To be sold at Public Auction

AT THE

SQUADRON "A" ARMORY

94th STREET and MADISON AVENUE

NEW YORK CITY

ON

December 10 and 11, 1924

Sale Starts Promptly at 7:30 P. M.

FASIG-TIPTON COMPANY

NEW YORK CITY

Gilt-edged catalog of the 1924 Xalapa Farm dispersal.

ers' Cup events. When I type in a web search, I stumble onto a twenty-two-minute-long film produced by British *Pathé* (which I self-consciously remind myself to pronounce with *l'accent aigu*). The film features a cameo by Belmont. Grandfather's famous boss fumbles with his field glasses as a cameraman whispers:

"Major Belmont, pretend you are watching a race through your binoculars."

All I've ever seen of Belmont are frozen-faced photographs. They prove no match for the *Pathé* footage of Belmont watching Zev defeat Papyrus. When he turns to the camera, a certain kindness shines in his eyes, as though he recognizes me. "You're Adolphe's grandson, aren't you?"

When the dead come to life, be it in books or photos or films, it's like some parlor trick. Bibliophiles call it the "momentum of imagination." Philosophers call it the "learning paradox." That you know enough to fill in some blanks. That you can't learn anything unless you already know something.

Oh, it's a paradox, all right. It's how this oddball example of archival whimsy triggers my imagination. Belmont's favorite polo pony is named Brick. When Brick dies, Belmont sends the horse's two front feet to a silversmith, who re-shoes the hard hooves into a pen-and-inkwell set.

The provenance of *le pieds* is as follows: Belmont's widow Eleanor presents the inkwell set to Grandfather, who leaves it to his son Uncle Johnny, who leaves it to his son John, who is my first cousin, and who presents the feet to me in my unofficial role as family historian. The inkwell is inscribed:

MY POLO PONY "BRICK"
DIED OCT. 1890
Aged 29 Years
The Gamest Piece of Horse Flesh For His Size I Ever Owned

When I google up a portrait of Belmont in a burgundy polo shirt astride Brick in the 1880s, I feel as though I've seen the shirt somewhere. From a vintage dome-topped trunk here in the attic, I pull out a well-worn, mildly moth-eaten woolen polo shirt. Same maroon stripe. The number "3" on the back. For a fleeting moment in the attic, I smell horse sweat and leather boots. I bend at the waist and cup my hand to give ghost-Augie a leg up on ghost-Brick to ride out onto the polo field for one last

Brick's pen-and-inkwell set.

chukker, for old time's sake. Just holding the ancient hooves in my hands prompts me to calculate their age. Brick wore his hooves for almost thirty years. Add another 130 since the silversmith tapped out the inkwell inscription. Brick's fossilized feet gotta be 160 years old.

ALL THAT GLITTERS

A line in a letter by poet Robert Lowell: "Everything that is isn't."

I feel this way about the Belmont family, beginning at their beginning in America. From the outside, they live the opulent life of the Gilded Age. But everything that is, isn't. I pour through David Black's *The King of Fifth Avenue: The Fortunes of August Belmont.* Black writes that Belmont's family in Germany—in the custom of Jewish families of the eighteenth century—were known by their given names and by their father's name. Enough to identify households. That the adopted surname of Belmont is French for "beautiful mountain." No such idyllic setting in real life. August Belmont, Sr. and his wife Caroline Slidell Perry Belmont lose a daughter, Pauline Jane ("Jeannie") to rheumatoid arthritis at age nineteen in 1875, and a son, Raymond, to suicide at age twenty-one in 1887.

Raymond's story is heartbreaking. He is an exuberant spoiled child, an entitled adult. After a winter's night carousing the social clubs of Manhattan, he returns to the family's Fifth Avenue mansion. It is after midnight when he goes down into the vast basement for some target practice in the mansion's shooting gallery. As a night-watchman runs to close the gallery door, he hears a pistol shot. Next morning's *New York Times*:

February 1, 1887:

> The watchman informed Mr. August Belmont. The shock completely prostrated him, and he was unable to leave his room.

The watchman said Raymond accidentally died. The coroner averred suicide. What was family life like in the Belmont mansion after this? People so rich they have a shooting gallery in their basement? Now their son's blood is down those stairs? The guilt of Gilded Age excess, on that doorstep. Caroline withdraws from society, shelters away at BytheSea.

Nor does it stop there. August Belmont II, on top of losing his brother Raymond and his sister Jeannie, loses his wife in 1896: Bessie Morgan Belmont dies on a trip to Paris at age thirty-six. She leaves behind August II and their three children: August III, Raymond, and Morgan.

Family tragedies beset every generation of Belmonts. In 1919, namesake August III dies from sepsis following routine surgery. He leaves behind a widow and five children, including August IV (who seventy-three years later will own 1983 Belmont Stakes winner Caveat). The oft-sad history of the Belmont family is revealed in Grandfather's letters, in *New York Times* archives, in biographies here in the attic. I read an account in Dan M. Bowmar III's *Giants of the Turf*:

> On Tuesday, December 9, 1924, August Belmont II went to his office in downtown New York. About noon he complained of a slight pain in his right arm, and told Adolphe Pons, his secretary for many years, to cancel his appointments.

Belmont dies of a blood clot thirty-six hours later. Upon the news, Kane mourns to Grandfather:

> Dear Mr. Pons,
> I always associated the horses with him and when one got sick or hurt, I always felt as if Major Belmont was present and helping us to pull them through. Yesterday I tried to feel the same, but it seemed as if the horses were strangers to me and they were of no significance.

Into mind come lines by poet Robert Frost:

> So Eden sank to grief,
> So dawn goes down to day.
> Nothing gold can stay.

FACTS

Grandfather is thrown into the chaos of the Belmont estate, the distress sale of the Nursery Stud horses. He is asked to advise the lawyers of Cadwalader, Wickersham & Taft, the firm of former President William Howard Taft. Colonel C. W. Wickersham paperclips a handwritten note to a folder: "Pons can give facts." Four words of deference. At stake, Belmont's most valuable assets. Six weeks after his death, creditors own his horses. I find this bill of sale:

MEMORANDUM FOR COLONEL WICKERSHAM
ESTATE OF AUGUST BELMONT

Agreement made 28th day of January 1925. Between Executors and Joseph E. Widener, to sell:

HORSES

A. Three Stallions known as
FAIR PLAY
HOURLESS and
MESSENGER
and
Sixty-three (63) mares
Price: $370,400

B. Twenty-six (26) Yearlings
Price: $110,000

Total: $480,000

The private sale price of Man o' War's sire Fair Play, of 1917 Belmont Stakes winner Hourless, of the entire Belmont broodmare band and the entire Nursery yearling crop, well exceeded Widener's $250,000 promissory note executed by the departed Belmont.

On Friday, May 15, 1925, seven days after the Preakness Stakes and one day before the Kentucky Derby—before the Triple Crown series was run in its present order of the Derby, the Preakness, and the Belmont—Widener resells the Belmont horses. From a black safety deposit box, I withdraw a yellowed seven-by-nine-inch envelope.

Catalog
of
Dispersal
Sale
of the
Famous
Nursery
Stud

Lexington, Ky.
May 15, 1925

But the envelope does not contain the catalog. Instead, I find Grandfather's receipts from staging the sale, the expenses of an event that fed three thousand guests—all that Kentucky fried chicken, all that burgoo and bourbon. I lick my fingers, dusty from the century-old records. I come upon ledger sheets of registered bidders, of prominent breeders adding Belmont's mares to their bands: Mrs. S. D. Riddle, Marshall Field, Gifford A. Cochran, James Cox Brady's Hamilton Farms, Walter J. Salmon, E. B. McLean. Finally, I find the actual catalog. On the cover: portraits of August Belmont I in a top hat, August Belmont II in a fedora. The terms:

WITHOUT RESERVE
by order of
JOSEPH E. WIDENER

Appointed as co-managers of the historic auction are Grandfather and the well-known auctioneer C. J. Fitzgerald. A brittle press clipping falls from the catalog:

Dateline Lexington, Ky., May 15
Special Dispatch to
The Morning Telegraph
FAIR PLAY SOLD
FOR $100,000

Nursery Stud Auction Sets
World's Record With $782,000
Total and $11,500 Average

Horses Widener bought in January for just under a half-million dollars appreciate by three hundred thousand dollars come May. Widener authorizes Grandfather to bid-in Fair Play—to "buy him back"—despite the "Without Reserve" assurance. Let's be precise: This was not a dispersal of Belmont's horses, but a resale of Widener's recent purchases. Widener also bids-in Man o' War's fifteen-year-old dam Mahubah, for seven thousand dollars. I research Mahubah's produce record; no foal in the five years from 1921 to 1925, as noted by Grandfather's penciled status reports in the catalog margins.

Missed
Missed
Missed
Missed
Missed

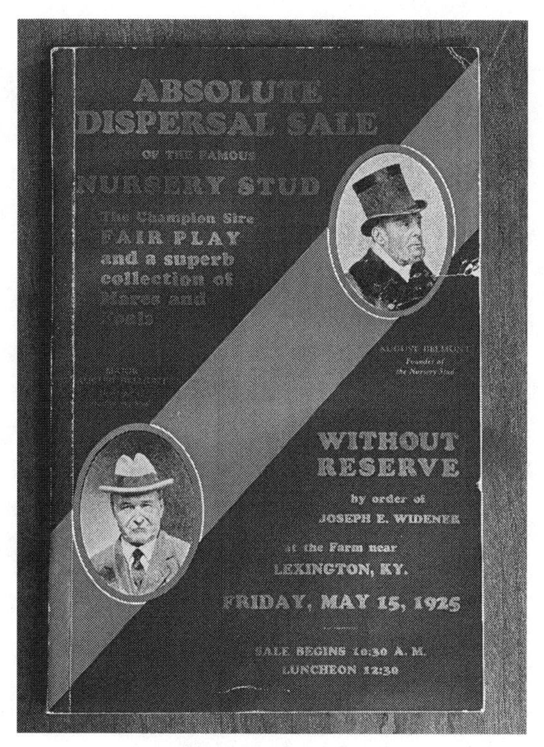

Nursery Stud dispersal catalog.

A veterinarian's assurance appears in the introduction to the catalog:

> While Mahubah has been barren for several seasons, Dr. Mc-Closkey believes she is now fertile and will produce.

Guess what? Mahubah never produces another live foal. I slide these century-old records gently back into the safety deposit box, but not before I've negligently exposed negatives to sunlight after one hundred years of darkness. I return my nattily dressed grandfather to an ancient manila sleeve so dry it breaks in my hands. It hurts me to hurt history. Why am I such a disturbance?

GRAPHOLOGY

Whenever I see Grandfather's signature, I pause. As distinctive as the era's Coca-Cola logo. Spencerian script. Fountain-pen penmanship. Elementary in the 1890s primary schools.

Grandfather's signature.

Grandfather learns at the feet of the Marist Brothers of St. Ann's Academy at Lexington and 76th Street. A French order of Catholic priests, the Marist Brothers drill the young French immigrant in bookkeeping terms dear to banker Belmont's heart: cash, property, promissory note, money-on-account. His notebooks record lessons in Morse code, dots and dashes on the exams. Today, as I sifted through files that contained his signature, I threw away bank statements from the 1920s. But some inner voice interceded, some inner attic eye stared into the recycle box. "Not so fast, kid." I glanced down into the discard bin and saw a check to Louie Feustel amid bills for maintenance of the Nursery Stud, for fencing, roofing, plumbing, electricity, fertilizer—the same as today's farm expenses.

I held the Feustel check up to the desk light. It was hole-punched by the bank: $25 PAID 10:7:26. I imagined hearing the smooth swish of Grandfather's pen banking ink into his distinctively oval *A*, into his circular *P*, but I felt silly reading too much into the confident style of his signature. His ghost doles out insight sparingly. I don't like getting ahead of him.

FAR FROM THE MADDEN CROWD

Ever sat in an empty house and thought you heard faint voices? Like a radio has been left on? Or a television two floors down, droning away?

Faint voices cause me to pause in my writing. Long seconds pass. My laptop senses inattention, defaults to auto-scroll through one-hundred-year-old photographs digitized for me by Coyle Studios in Baltimore. I hear voices, ancestral uncles—young men in the earliest days of Country Life. They are teenagers leaping onto birdbath pedestals, riding ponies bareback, clowning for Kodaks, wriggling on the lawn with the latest litter of puppies.

Some voice-over narration happens when I enter this empty old farmhouse, south-facing to the morning sun, the direction old-time farmers oriented their homesites for warmth. Artwork comes to life. Shafts of light reflect off Belmont's framed photographs of Epsom Derby winner Flying Fox, of Ascot Gold Cup winner St. Simon—identification portraits required by the English Jockey Club. In the hall above the bar with the brass footrail, Fair Play strikes his conformation photo. Mahubah's father Rock Sand strides out in the silks of English breeder Sir James Miller. Rock Sand's dad Sainfoin rides high above a fireplace. Grandfather's first stallion at Country Life, Ladkin, stares upstairs to Richard Stone Reeves' conformation print of Man o' War: Both are sons of Fair Play.

This moldy old house, its arches of stained glass windows suffusing light, is filled with images of these famous Thoroughbreds. When my imagination seizes me, the stairwells echo with voices and the horses on the walls race back to life, galloping faster and faster and faster like those silhouettes in Eadweard Muybridge's zoopraxiscope. Then it's quiet and lonely once more in the empty farmhouse.

I never dreamt I would work in such august company of horses and horsemen. Hello John Madden. He resides in his own private set of Gaylord archival storage boxes, just as he resided in his own private suite at the Hotel Pennsylvania in New York City, across Seventh Avenue from Pennsylvania Station. Madden's spirit rises out of books he authored, out of pedigrees of his expansive broodmare band, out of Hamburg Place Stud invoices to Belmont, marked PAID from lively trade in Fair Play blood. On the cover of *BloodHorse* of November 9, 1929, Madden appears waxy faced in a studio portrait. The headline of his obituary reads simply:

THE WIZARD DIES

Death-defying catchlight in his eyes. Wool suit, fedora, bowtie, kerchief. Dress rehearsal for an open casket. Editor Thomas B. Cromwell:

Eleven years he had been the leading breeder of Thoroughbreds in America.

Letters on all-caps HOTEL PENNSYLVANIA stationery show how the Wizard conducted his business.

October 20, 1927

Mr. Adolphe Pons
45 Cedar St.
New York City

Dear Mr. Pons:
I am at the Race Track every day and I am sure you can't miss me. I have a number of pedigrees of brood mares to submit to you.

Yours very truly,
JEMadden

He publishes a private catalog listing 110 mares, eight stallions, including Man o' War's full brother Playfellow. In it, he tracks a Friar Rock mare named Harridan back to her twenty-fourth dam, the Layton Barb Mare, from the Bruce Lowe No. 4 Family. Harridan carries a brand on her shoulder: 333. Breeders with herds the size of Madden's often branded their horses as means of identification—should a halter nameplate fall off, should a farm manager familiar with the stock be hired away. This is a century before digital identification of Thoroughbreds, before a computer chip inserted by needle under a horse's mane assured identity: "This is the right horse."

To learn about Bruce Lowe's No. 4 Family, I pull down a burgundy book signed by Grandfather in 1913, *Breeding Racehorses by the Figure System*. I stare at a collage print of seventeenth-century foundation sires the Godolphin Barb, the Darley Arabian, and the Byerley Turk, distant headwaters of the Thoroughbred breed. I study portraits of their eighteenth-century descendant stallions Herod, Matchem, and Eclipse, to whom modern Thoroughbreds trace. The attic swirls in equine history. Take a breath. Focus on Madden's catalog:

PEDIGREES OF RACE HORSES
FOALED IN
England, France, and America
at

HAMBURG PLACE STUD
Lexington, Ky., U. S. A.

Madden writes as though he is parodying his contemporary Ernest Hemingway:

> The practical man need confine himself to the formula only of breeding a good mare to a great horse. . . . He will have his good years and his bad years, and the experts will tack figures on to the pedigrees of his winners and tell him how it all happened.

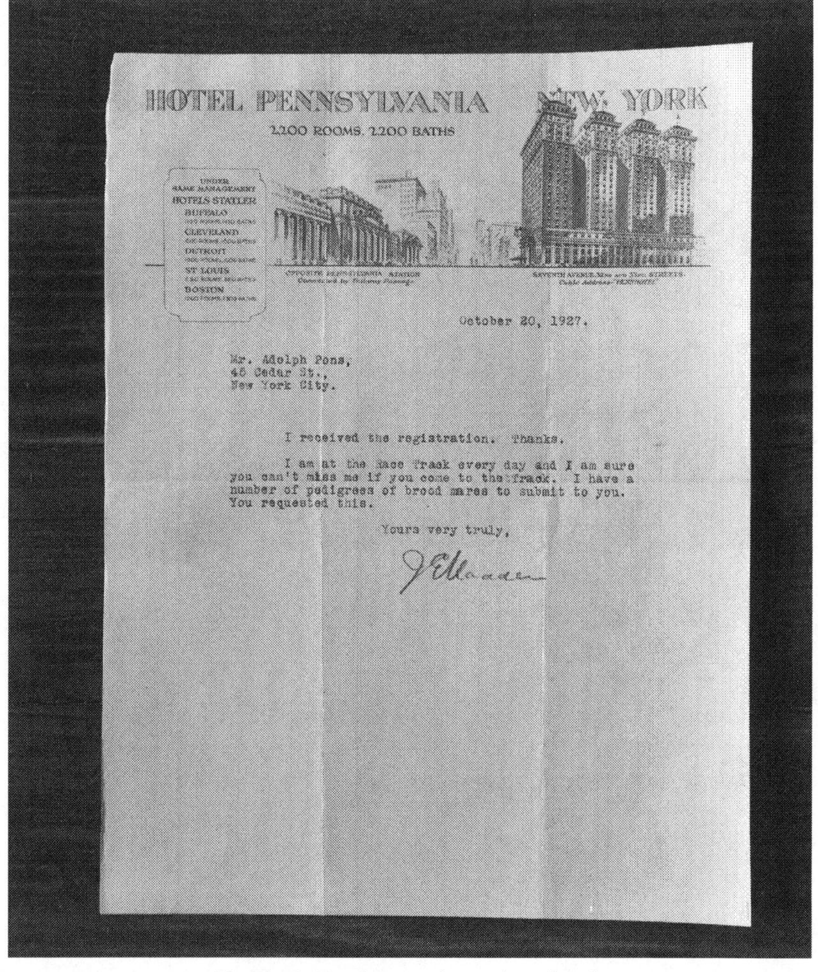

HOTEL PENNSYLVANIA NEW YORK
2200 ROOMS. 2200 BATHS

UNDER SAME MANAGEMENT
HOTELS STATLER
BUFFALO
CLEVELAND
DETROIT
ST LOUIS
BOSTON

October 20, 1927.

Mr. Adolph Pons,
46 Cedar St.,
New York City.

I received the registration. Thanks.

I am at the Race Track every day and I am sure you can't miss me if you come to the Track. I have a number of pedigrees of brood mares to submit to you. You requested this.

Yours very truly,

J E Madden

Madden's Hotel Pennsylvania letterheads.

The Hotel Pennsylvania letterhead boasts of twenty-two hundred rooms, with twenty-two hundred baths. All those rooms, for all those people, and this most famous of horsemen dies alone. No family nearby. No friends from the track. I can't shake that lonely image of Madden in that massive hotel, but dead is dead. I drop back down the stairs, pass beneath portraits of four-legged patron saints of the Thoroughbred kingdom and run out onto the farm, happy to see the living.

WRITER IN WONDERLAND

The Bible of the Turf may be William H. P. Robertson's *The History of Thoroughbred Racing in America.* Look here for Rancocas Stud, named for the Rancocas River. Opulent New Jersey farm of tobacco magnate Pierre Lorillard in the late 1800s, bought by oilman Harry F. Sinclair in the 1920s. Harry is the Sinclair of those gas stations out West with their cartoon green dinosaur logo. Fueled by oil money, he assembles the leading stable of his era. Writes Robertson on page 247:

> With all the enthusiasm of a child with a new toy, Sinclair was snapping up every horse that caught his fancy.

Sinclair hires Belmont's former trainer Sam Hildreth, then buys Mad Hatter, a son of Fair Play. Carrying the Rancocas silks, Mad Hatter is the 1921 champion older horse in America, the same season Sinclair and Hildreth win the Belmont Stakes with Grey Lag. In 1923, Sinclair's colors are in the Winner's Circle for both the Kentucky Derby and Belmont Stakes when Zev takes two of America's three classic races.

Robertson's Rancocas backstory sends me to Grandfather's files. Sealed away in the basement has been a 1940s brochure about Rancocas, when Grandfather advised then-owner William Helis, a Greek shipping magnate. The brochure opens with photos of Lorillard's enormous and elegant barns, renovated by Sinclair, as fields of yearlings stand at attention, heads over brand-new board fencing built in the Helis era.

In *New York Times*' archival articles from its online *Timesmachine* library, I read that Rancocas barns "occupied half a city block," and that on April 14, 1923, a month before Zev's May 19 Kentucky Derby win, fire levels two barns. Sixty horses burned alive. Cryptic headlines from *The Thoroughbred Record* magazine:

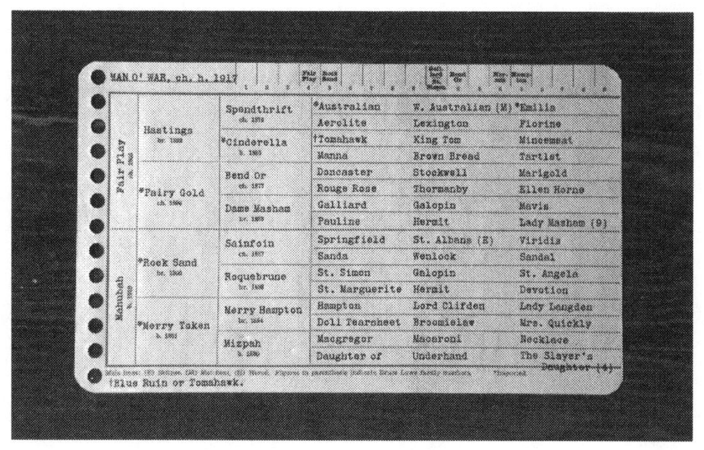

MAN O' WAR, ch. h. 1917

Fair Play	Hastings	Spendthrift	*Australian	W. Australian (M)	*Emilia
			Aerolite	Lexington	Florine
		*Cinderella	†Tomahawk	King Tom	Mincemeat
			Manna	Brown Bread	Tartlet
	*Fairy Gold	Bend Or	Doncaster	Stockwell	Marigold
			Rouge Rose	Thormanby	Ellen Horne
		Dame Masham	Galliard	Galopin	Mavis
			Pauline	Hermit	Lady Masham (9)
Mahubah	*Rock Sand	Sainfoin	Springfield	St. Albans (E)	Viridis
			Sanda	Wenlock	Sandal
		Roquebrune	St. Simon	Galopin	St. Angela
			St. Marguerite	Hermit	Devotion
	*Merry Token	Merry Hampton	Hampton	Lord Clifden	Lady Langden
			Doll Tearsheet	Broomielaw	Mrs. Quickly
		Mizpah	Macgregor	Macaroni	Necklace
			Daughter of	Underhand	The Slayer's Daughter (4)

†Blue Ruin or Tomahawk.

Man o' War pedigree.

```
Frenzied neighing
Ablaze in two places
Suspicion of incendiary origin
```

Among the dead is Inchcape, whom Sinclair had bought for $115,000, a huge swing at acquiring a foundation stallion for Rancocas. Inchcape was a son of Belmont's Belmont Stakes winner Friar Rock, who was by Rock Sand, who was the sire of Mahubah, who was the mother of Man o' War.

In Hildreth's boastful autobiography *Under the Spell of the Turf*, he writes how he prepared Zev for the ballyhooed contest against Papyrus in the first International Match Race.

"It is of Zev I tell," begins Hildreth, in windy braggadocio. He trains his horses hard: Elizabeth Kane confides to Grandfather that one bright aspect of Belmont having sold Man o' War is that the headstrong colt is handled by the patient Feustel, not the hardboot Hildreth.

Greenridge Cemetery in Saratoga is Hildreth's forever home, close enough for him to hear the cheers from the racecourse. As I close the covers of his autobiography, I pause at the frontispiece: a photo of the second of the three international contests in 1924. French champion Epinard nosed out by Ladkin. I can't even close a book without being spellbound. Grandfather snaps his fingers and I come back from far away: "Keep reading."

November 22nd, 1918

MEMORANDUM FOR MAJOR AUGUST BELMONT

Mr. Hildreth has returned to Belmont Park with his horses, including MAD HATTER.

Adolphe

Mad Hatter becomes a dot in an attic full of dots. On my walk home, I peer up into the night sky, into the chaos of stars. It's maddening—until you see how constellations connect. Just dots until you see the outline of mythological figures.

All I want to do is learn more about the stars of the 1920s. I need to run away for a day, to drive north to what little remains of New Jersey's farmland, see the spectacular ruins of Rancocas, let the sea-salt Atlantic breezes carry the sounds of history to me. I drive out of Maryland and cross the Delaware River into New Jersey, take the old Monmouth Road through tiny four-cornered Jobstown. On a flat stretch of Jersey farmland, I spot intact remains of the famed farm. Empty. Deserted. At the farm office, a note posted to the door reads: "Out on an Errand." I am the only living soul on grand old Rancocas. The black-slate roof of the Stallion Barn is inlaid with diamond-shaped red slate. Why, of course. Lorillard's racing silks were black and red. Hildreth exaggerates only slightly in his description of Rancocas:

A great estate of 1,244 acres. The training track, one mile and five-eighths in length.

The Rancocas training barns are so immense as to be irreparable: eleven hundred windows, hundreds of them vandalized into shards of glass. Acres of asbestos shingles have collapsed through rotten roofing to fall into triple-wide shedrows. How to block out the sad sight of a farm in irreversible decay? Close your eyes. Travel back to the 1800s. Do you see that handsome man in the pointy Victorian mustache? That's Pierre Lorillard, reaching into his vest for a gold stopwatch to clock a workout by Iroquois. In 1881, Iroquois will become the first American-bred racehorse to win the Epsom Derby.

Leap forward to the 1920s. That's Hildreth waving to riders for more speed in breezes by Kentucky Derby winners Grey Lag and Zev. Trip ahead to the 1940s. That's Grandfather arriving in his Packard for an appointment with Helis. I come full circle back to the present and say to all these ghosts on this vast lonely farm: "Hop in boys, we're going to Monmouth."

An hour later, the history lesson continues. The clubhouse wall at Monmouth Park displays portraits of New Jersey–bred Hall of Famers. There's August Belmont II's Henry of Navarre, America's Horse of the Year in 1894 and 1896, famous match-race nemesis of Domino. There's Harry Payne Whitney's 1915 Kentucky Derby–winning filly Regret, foaled at Whitney's Brookdale Farm right here in Monmouth County. There's Isabel Dodge Sloane's 1934 Kentucky Derby winner Cavalcade, foaled in Morristown.

"I know all of you," I say to the wall. "I've met you in the attic."

Monmouth regulars on their way to mutuel windows hear me talking to pictures, look at me like I'm as mad as a hatter.

FIRST CALL

Brass prongs secure a bale of letters: the 1920s Arden Farms file of the Harriman family. I risk tetanus as I bend the rusty rabbit-ears straight, then force them back through their hole-punched papers. For the first time in a hundred years, the bundle breathes. As fiscal agent for the Harrimans, Grandfather tactfully avoids a misunderstanding between the heirs to the Union Pacific Railroad and the future Hall of Fame rider Earl Sande.

Brass prongs secure a bale of letters.

March 10th, 1927

Mr. Earl Sande
Louisville, Kentucky

My dear Sande:

In looking over the Arden Farms account of 1926, I fail to find any payment made to you for your winning mount on Chance Play at Havre de Grace last Fall. I know it was Mr. Harriman's intention to give you a gratuity, but undoubtedly it escaped his notice.

Have you already signed for "second call?" I think they would like to get a call on your services for this year. With kindest regards,

Very truly yours,
Adolphe Pons

Top jockeys often signed under exclusive contracts to owners who paid them a fee for "first call" on their riding services or, as I have just learned, a "second call." A claim of priority. Like first dibs. A jockey's customary compensation of 10 percent was paid by owners from their own funds, by cash or check—not by automatic debit and credit through the horsemen's bookkeeper, as is the practice today. I find a statement in which Walter Salmon bridles at paying 10 percent, approves only 5 percent. Grandfather, as his fiscal agent, is caught between a jock and a hard case. He makes up the missing 5 percent out of his own pocket.

After Chance Play earns twenty-five thousand dollars at Lincoln Fields, Grandfather follows up with Arden Farms treasurer W. L. Pemberton, Esq.:

Kindly send Earl Sande a check for $2,500—unless you have already done so.

The first call for Sande's services belongs to Widener; second call to Riddle, owner of Man o' War's champion son Crusader. Harriman doesn't have a large stable. But he has one very good horse: Chance Play. Sande writes to Harriman from The Brown Hotel in Louisville, Kentucky.

```
March 25, 1927

Dear Mr. Harriman:
  Chance Play earned $13,250 from his win at Havre de Grace
and $2,000 for his second to Crusader at Laurel.
  Mr. Riddle asked me about a second call for this year at
Pimlico last fall. If he has decided not to train Crusader,
he probably won't want me.

                                          Sincerely yours,
                                               Earl Sande
```

When I slide old metal paperclips off top pages, their rusted imprints remain. Perfect red ovals the shape of tiny racetracks. Subliminal effect: How small the world of Thoroughbred racing was back then. Overlaps abound. Sande wins the 1927 Belmont Stakes with Chance Play's full brother Chance Shot for Widener; Grandfather is on retainer to Widener, to Harriman, to Riddle. Conflicts of interest are disclosed.

The same *Daily Racing Form* that carries news of Chance Shot's Belmont victory carries sidebars of other news of the day. The Illinois Oaks at Washington Park is won by Yeddo, owned by the Waggoner family's Three D's Stock Farm Stable of Texas, to whom Grandfather will one day sell his entire 1935 weanling crop; second in that Illinois Oaks is a filly

Country Life's first crop of foals bought by Waggoner Farm, 1935.

named Mary Jane, winner of the 1927 Kentucky Oaks, and for whom Grandfather is dispatched to Chicago by Mrs. Kitty Harriman to purchase.

It feels as though the entire sport of racing takes place in the lobby of a mythical Algonquin Hotel, where every deal is written down in letters, telegrams, handwritten marginalia edifying the moment. All the sifting and sorting of correspondence between jockeys, owners, trainers, agents, advisors. What a time capsule of correspondence I've stumbled upon, exhuming it from the basement, examining it in the attic.

TELEPATHY

A scholarly book entitled *The Library at Night*, by Alberto Manguel. Essays on the enduring need for libraries. Chapters stitched together with one-word titles: The Library as Order . . . as Workshop . . . as Chance . . . as Imagination . . . as Identity. Manguel writes that a library contains "vast potencies of telepathic communication." That's this room, cluttered now in a profusion of artists and authors. Insistent voices rattle the windows of this library at night.

Painter George Stubbs says he lived in a tannery to skin away layers of hide, to understand how to depict a horse. Franklin Voss explains how he portrayed muscular Man o' War as though the horse was a Greek god. Henry M. Shrady, sculptor of the Grant Memorial below the steps of the US Capitol building, dissected horses at the Museum of Natural History before rendering an entire cavalry in bronze.

Books lean on photos on desks laden with letters and lists. Grandfather shows me his typewritten record of the Mereworth Stud racing stable he leased in 1932 and 1933. My hands land on a photo, a three-quarter pose—just the massive shoulder, just the blaze-face of the great champion Discovery, who raced in Grandfather's purple silks thirteen times as a two-year-old. Here's the 1936 volume of *American Racehorses*. John Hervey cites Greek poet Homer in sixteen enlightening pages detailing the odyssey of Discovery. Dead poets talk to dead authors about dead horses in this room of endless discovery.

Every picture tells a story. Grandfather sits on a racetrack bench with Gwyn R. Tompkins, who trained 1925 Belmont Stakes winner American Flag, a colt from Man o' War's first crop of foals. I reach for volumes of *Racing in America*. Find a picture of American Flag, of whom Hervey writes:

Pons and Gwyn Tompkins.

American Flag in both appearance and manner recalled Man o' War himself.

Letter from Grandfather to Man o' War's owner:

Samuel D. Riddle, Esq., N.Y., 1926

My dear Mr. Riddle:
It is understood that you will give me a complimentary service to AMERICAN FLAG for next year. If at any time I come across another bargain, such as MAN O' WAR, when I brought him to your attention as a yearling, I will be glad to let you have first chance.

Over and over, telepathy at work. Find a photo. Find a book. Find a letter. Find the thread.

FOREBODING

Grandfather is forty-two years old in 1925 when he receives this report from the Life Extension Institute—its very name a bold claim.

Mr. Adolphe A. Pons
16 Elm Street
Garden City, L.I., N.Y.

Weight - 135 pounds
Blood pressure - sys. 110, dias. 80

Our examiner reports a slight change in your heart action, that you have a low blood pressure and rapid pulse. This calls for further investigation, as this may yield information of decided benefit. Have your doctor examine your circulatory apparatus three or four times a year.

Grandfather lowers his head into his hands and whispers: "My poor apparatus." That year of 1925, he is likewise heartsick at how quickly creditors descend on the Belmont estate. The prized Nursery Stud blood had served as unrecorded collateral for Belmont's debts on the subway construction. For decades, New York City transit officials refused Belmont's plea to raise the 1904 nickel fare. To ride anywhere and everywhere, no matter the distance, cost only a nickel. It won't be until 1948 that the fare doubles to a dime. The Cape Cod Canal further bled Belmont. Cruel timing, the ribbon-cutting on the eve of the Great War, German U-Boats harrying merchant vessels.

Thoroughbred horses were Belmont's most liquid assets, and creditors claimed them. Grandfather sees firsthand the harsh treatment of an underfunded estate. In the coming years, he takes measures to protect his own modest holdings. In 1932, he writes to The Prudential:

Following is a list of policies on my life:

Equitable	$3,000
Union Central	$10,000
Metropolitan	$10,000
New York Life	$5,000
Mutual Life	$40,000

By this time, he is trying to keep his head above the waves of the Great Depression. He carries five policies of life insurance in the event his "apparatus" fails. He is almost maniacally active. "Glad to the brink of fear," as Emerson wrote. I read into Grandfather's mindset: "How long have I got? What will I leave my family?"

RISKY BUSINESS

It's 1932. A great economic crisis paralyzes the country. In sporting news, the headlines read:

Breeders Suffer by Low Prices at Saratoga

This depressing year, Col. Phil T. Chinn averaged $1,004 for 62 yearlings,
contrasted with $2,811 a year ago.

Since Belmont's dispersal in 1925, Grandfather has served as an aide-to-camp to wealthy horse breeders: Averell Harriman's Arden Farms, George Herbert Walker's Log Cabin Stud, Samuel D. Riddle's Glen Riddle Farms, Isabel Dodge Sloane's Brookmeade Stable, Harry Sinclair's Rancocas Stable, Walter J. Salmon's Mereworth Stud. His reputation for honesty, his talent as a fastidious clerk, assures him of retainers. He records minutiae for inclusion in *The Racing Calendar*—a monthly registry published by The Jockey Club. He double checks that his clients' racing silks are unique, unlike any others, as he pays to register them as "Life Colors." A notable example, the satin silks worn aboard Man o' War:

GLEN RIDDLE FARMS—Black, yellow sash, yellow bars on sleeves

Grandfather corrects errata on foal certificates, maintains nominations for rich two-year-old races known as futurities, files forms for ASSUMED NAMES, forms for AUTHORIZED AGENTS. He commutes into Manhattan from his tidy home at 16 Elm Street in Garden City, boarding the Long Island Railroad at the Doubleday Printing Company's Country Life Press station stop. He fantasizes about naming a farm Country Life someday, considers moving to Maryland with his wife Mary, their four children Addie, Johnny, Marie, and Joseph. A fifth child, Lucy E., is listed among family interments at Calvary Cemetery. Born Jan. 4, 1911. Age at death: 1 Day. Stillborn? A mystery, reminding me of Hemingway's six-word short story: "For Sale. Baby Shoes. Never Worn."

The summer of 1932, Grandfather gets a taste of big-time racehorse ownership. He writes to young horse trainer Jack Pryce with precise instructions:

July 1, 1932

Dear Jack:

Mr. Salmon has decided to retire from racing and the horses, therefore, cannot run in the Mereworth Stud name. I have leased all the horses you have at Arlington Park and accepted their engagements under a percentage agreement with Mr. Salmon.

Beginning on Wednesday, July 6th, you will, therefore, start all horses in my name and under my racing colors of purple with gold shoulder braces and purple cap. All arrangements you had with Mr. Salmon will be carried out by me. I have filed a transfer of engagements with the Arlington Association and the Illinois Turf Association.

I hope you and I can make it a go on the racing stable and more than pay expenses, which I feel sure of. Wishing you the best of luck,

Adolphe Pons

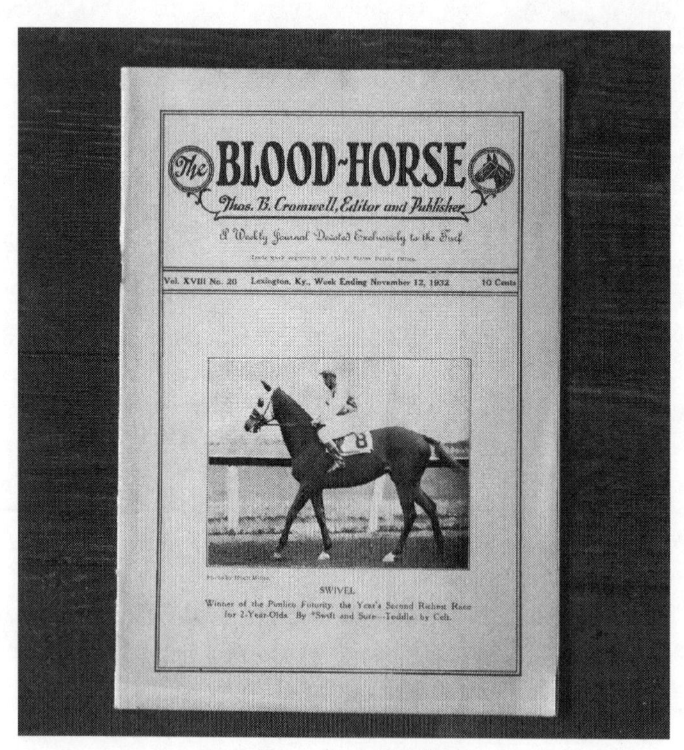

The BLOOD-HORSE

Thos. B. Cromwell, Editor and Publisher

A Weekly Journal Devoted Exclusively to the Turf

Vol. XVIII No. 20 Lexington, Ky., Week Ending November 12, 1932 10 Cents

SWIVEL

Winner of the Pimlico Futurity, the Year's Second Richest Race for 2-Year-Olds. By *Swift and Sure—Toddle, by Celt.

Swivel featured in BloodHorse.

Six months later, he is writing to Major Belmont's widow about the risks he took.

December 6th, 1932

Mrs. Eleanor R. Belmont
1115 Fifth Avenue
New York City

My dear Mrs. Belmont:
I have never worked so hard in my life, and have done plenty of worrying, but I am happy to say that I made a success with a stable our friends thought I was foolish to take over. I have actively handled the horses I had under lease from Mr. Salmon. I won the Pimlico Futurity with SWIVEL, and the Endurance Stakes with PROJECTILE, who is out of the old Nursery mare Fair Priscilla. I had to take a chance for the sake of my family.

An accounting sheet arrives from Mereworth just in time for Christmas.

December 15th, 1932

From: Mereworth Stud
To: Adolphe Pons

10% of winnings of racing stable for 1932 above $100,000, as per agreement:
Winnings, as per attached list: $118,745.
10% of $18,745 = $1,874

His optimism for the coming racing season is apparent in this letter to former Nursery Stud veterinarian Dr. Frank Wehle:

My dear Doc Wehle:
I think I have two good prospective 3-year-olds for 1933. Wouldn't it be great if I could win a Preakness? But believe me I sweat blood all summer wondering how I would make out.

How close to the sun he is about to become. This objective report appears in *BloodHorse* of April 29, 1933, just days before the Kentucky Derby:

> Adolphe Pons' Swivel is the leading filly candidate for the Derby, and many experienced horsemen believe she will take her place alongside Regret as a winner of the classic. She is a stronger, bigger, more masculine sort. On April 22, she made her first start since winning the Pimlico Futurity, and won in effortless fashion.

Lyrics of a bittersweet song play: *Riding high in April, shot down in May.* The Derby slips away. The harsh nature of the horse business asserts itself. I find these letters:

> May 2nd, 1933
>
> Dear Mr. Pons:
> I was terribly sorry to learn of Swivel's illness but hope that if she cannot make the Derby she will at least go in the Preakness.
>
> Frank J. Brady
> Treasurer Maryland State Fair

> June 13th, 1933
>
> My dear Doc. Wehle:
> We have had the damndest luck possible with SWIVEL. She took that coughing epidemic.
>
> Adolphe

> June 21st, 1933
>
> Glencrest Stock Farm
> R. H. Farmer
> Midway, Kentucky
>
> My dear Mr. Pons:
> It is very unfortunate that both SWIVEL and PROJECTILE should have gotten sick. Especially SWIVEL. I really expected her to beat most of the three-year-olds this year.
>
> R. H. Farmer

WALKING IN THEIR FOOTSTEPS

Cellphone screen saver is a black-and-white photograph of 1927 Belmont Stakes winner Chance Shot, from a photo on the wall in the Belmont Park Clubhouse. He is striding back to the Winner's Circle under Earl Sande, whose hands relax on the buckle of the reins. The two could be returning from a fox hunt. Famed photographer C. C. Cook anticipated when one of Chance Shot's forelegs would be fully extended—a display of grace simply by walking. Same stride captured in a photo of American Flag in 1925, of Crusader in 1926. Look-alikes, big-boned types. Three Belmont Stakes winners in a row. I stood on tiptoe to take photos of Cook's photos, reaching for 1920s horses I knew scant about until my graduate course in horse history, these attic lessons in century-old letters, books, photos.

Chance Shot was the full brother to Grandfather's favorite stallion Chance Play, who was 1927 Horse of the Year. Both were sons of foundation sire Fair Play, whose sire was 1896 Belmont Stakes winner Hastings, in turn whose sire was 1879 Belmont Stakes winner Spendthrift. Fair Play's most famous son, of course, was 1920 Belmont Stakes winner Man o' War, who sired American Flag and Crusader. All these winners of the famous Belmont Stakes, all with the same walk, all along the walls of Belmont Park.

Horse racing roars through the 1920s, crashes into the 1930s. Grandfather describes those difficult years in a letter to his sister in France, their brother Etienne suddenly jobless.

February 5th, 1931

My dear Marie Jeanne:

The stock market is very bad, dividends cut or omitted altogether. Unemployment runs into millions. We are in a depression that it will take a long time to get over.

To make things worse, the Country is suffering from lack of rain. Ponds, brooks, and wells have gone dry, and the crops destroyed. Out West in the farming section the people are starving.

Etienne has been laid off as a clerk at August Belmont & Co. who are on the rocks, and ready to close its doors.

I am always rushed and thank God for that. But the trips are beginning to get tiresome. I go to Kentucky and Virginia every month. I really look after too much, but I have some very good customers.

It is a gentleman's game, and you come into contact with all the biggest people in the Country.

I do not feel old, but maybe Adolphe could take this up after he gets out of school. When I look at the children, I begin to think.

Affectionately yours,
Adolphe

It is exhausting being a horse salesman when no one is buying. I carefully lift out a ragged-edged carbon of a letter from 1932—translucent, browned and curled, as though once held too close to heat. Fragile paper fibers preserve the sharp tone of the letter. Grandfather is selling hard—hoping to lease one of his broodmares to a stockbroker who has secured a rare outside-the-Riddle-camp breeding nomination to Man o' War.

Mr. T. W. Durant
E. F. Hutton & Co.
New York City

My dear Mr. Durant:

If you are looking for a well-bred mare to suit MAN O' WAR, here she is:

POND LILY, by Ultimus.

If you do not lease her, this mare is booked to the best FAIR PLAY horse in America, CHANCE PLAY, and do not come back in three years and say that I did not tell you.

What a bold prediction, yet he's right. Chance Play does in fact lead the national 1935 General Sire list, then repeats the feat in 1944, at age twenty-one. For Mrs. Averell Harriman's account, Grandfather stands Chance Play at the farm where the colt was born in 1923, Grandfather having assumed the lease on Belmont's Nursery Stud, now doing business as Greenwich Stud.

In 1936, he arranges the sale of Chance Play from Mrs. Harriman to Warren Wright's Calumet Farm for seventy thousand dollars. A promotional brochure for Chance Play falls from a folder, crisp as if printed yesterday, bearing the distinctive red Calumet Farm logo of an Indian chief in feathered head-dress. I hold Grandfather's letter imploring Wall Street broker Durant to take a chance on his mare booked to Chance Play. His pitch to Durant hangs in the attic air:

Please let me know at once regarding the above matter, as Pond Lily is due to foal in the next two weeks.

With kind regards,
Adolphe Pons

Poor hesitant Durant will come to regret his lack of faith. Grandfather saw the horse business for what it is: a game of chance. Just keep playing. The Great Depression may grip the country, but he is certain happier days lie just ahead.

Chance Play brochure.

JUST A MINUTE

Today's horse business is not memorialized on hotel letterhead but on ethereal stationery: texts, emails, Instagrams. Letters won't be found in attics in coming years. Our voices won't carry. Who will keep the everyday records that a century from now will bear witness to history? Today's electronic messages seem banal compared to attic communiques. Who would know the inside story of Chance Play, the 1927 Horse of the Year, a stallion my grandfather once stood in Kentucky, who shuttles to the Adirondacks of New York just as he is emerging as the leading sire in the country, which prompts his return to the Bluegrass, where he does it again at Calumet Farm. I knew none of this until I found primary source letters preserved for decades in the basement of a Maryland farmhouse.

My dear Mrs. Harriman:

Following is the amount won by the various horses, the property of the Arden Farms, for the year 1927:

Chance Play	$85,275
Claptrap	$300
Hat Brush	$700
Sun Edwin	$1,500
Mary Jane	$7,250
TOTAL:	$95,025

I sincerely hope that next year every horse in the stable will be on the winning list.

Sincerely yours,
Adolphe Pons

Without documents down the ages, I would have missed history's perfect example of how one good racehorse, a Chance Play, can carry an entire stable. The digital era will bear no such witness. History will be silent.

CRACK OF THE CUE BALL

Maryland's Harford County in 1933 is a Garden of Eden, full of industrious dairy farms, full of cedar-laned horse farms. Stands of virgin mid-Atlantic hardwood forests. Tulip poplars measuring five feet in diameter. Country roads bordered by apple orchards. Splendid farmhouses. The night sky a brilliant planetarium. And, happily for Grandfather, a train runs through it, back and forth to New York City. He is smitten by the beauty of Harford County. When he examines bank lists of some thirty Maryland farms forced onto the market by unmet mortgages, he narrows the list to farms not remote from train stations. That's this county. He wants a closer look.

April 10th, 1933
Manager, Lord Baltimore Hotel

Dear Sir:
As I generally stay at your hotel when I am down during the racing season, I hope you will let me have three nice rooms. With my wife and children, we will be six in the party.

The Maryland Horse Breeders Association has just published *Maryland and the Thoroughbred* by D. Sterett Gittings. Governor Albert Ritchie has written the foreword:

Our accessibility renders Maryland an ideal place for carrying on this most important industry of raising Thoroughbreds.

In America in 1933, the average male life expectancy is fifty-eight years. Grandfather is forty-nine. His heart, before the term atrial fibrillation was coined, beats in irregular tremors. He hears it when his head rests on pillows and intuitively understands he has no time to lose. About him flows an urgency, a determination to leave a better life for his family. Midsummer, he takes the train to Maryland, hops off at Aberdeen, rents a car, drives through the tidy little town of Bel Air, the county seat. An imposing red-brick courthouse—Italianate style, dome-topped, built in 1858—anchors Main Street. Just across from the courthouse are the steep steps of the Vaughn Hotel, home to Preston's Stationery Store, where he buys the *Morning Telegraph*, checks New York's race entries and results, wishes it were the local racing season at nearby Havre de Grace Race Track, where he watched Man o' War win the Potomac Handicap a dozen years back. One floor below the newsstand, pool sharks crack cue balls on slate-bottomed tables in Preston's basement. Life is a gamble.

Grandfather is about to buy a one-hundred-acre farm two miles south of Bel Air, on a hill looking down on Route 1. He has eliminated the idea of buying a farm in Kentucky—too far from his New York clients. He has driven around Maryland, examined ground, walked into and out of a dozen farmhouses, shooed off real estate men desperate to sell. The farm he has found is perfect. A fine manor house with arching stained glass windows, handsome shingle-style architecture, ornate balconies, white columns on wraparound porches.

And for the fine Thoroughbreds to come? Why, spring water flows through all the big fields, the pastures are lush green, and the hills are perfect for developing young equine athletes. Driving down across the bridge over scenic Lake Fanny above the rapids of Winters Run, Grandfather eyes his future home. A clipping from September of 1933 in the Harford County newspaper, *The Aegis*:

> Mr. Adolphe Pons, long associated with the late August Belmont, has purchased the old David and Ralph Charles Lee farm. The 100-acre tract is right on the Bel Air Road. The amount is said to be $20,000 from Raymond D. Miller, a retired minister.

The Lees, a Quaker family, owned farms on roads with names from the Bible—Joppa, Jerusalem, Jericho—and to power the waterwheels of their mills, always near rivers—Big Gunpowder, Little Gunpowder, Winters Run. They masoned fieldstone footers twenty-feet high on which to construct their elaborate barns, hand-hewn timbers mortised and tenoned, rising forty feet into the sky.

The Lees sold Rockland Farm to Miller in 1917, the Great War ramping up. Miller sold Rockland sixteen years later to Grandfather, the Great Depression descending.

T. S. ELIOT

Paper-thin hearts beat in these letters. Sometimes I am afraid to take their pulse. What if I don't get their stories right? T. S. Eliot felt similar trepidation in his poem "J. Alfred Prufrock."

> Do I dare? Do I dare? Time to turn back and descend the stair.

If I don't dare, I'll miss messages from Grandfather. And so I dig back in, find a letter he wrote to an old friend, Hall of Fame trainer A. J. Joyner. It was Joyner who sailed to Europe to train 1912 St. Leger Stakes winner Tracery for Belmont. In his dotage, the venerable trainer serves as racing manager for the fashionable George D. Widener stable. Joyner has what Grandfather needs: a stallion to attract business.

> November 27th, 1933
>
> My dear Mr. Joyner:
> I was wondering if you would consider standing JAMESTOWN in Maryland this coming year. As you know, I have purchased a farm outside of Bel Air. Easily accessible. Hard roads lead right to the stables. With bonuses offered for Maryland-bred horses, we will have a very good selection of stallions in the State.

Jamestown is a five-year-old former champion juvenile colt, winner of the rich Futurity three seasons back for Joyner, and sired by St. James—also a two-year-old champion, also a Futurity winner. Out of a mare by Fair Play, a pedigree right up Belmont-alley for Grandfather. Jamestown is everything Grandfather could ask for in a stallion, so he asks Joyner, who asks his boss Widener, who politely declines. Sixty miles north of Country Life, Jamestown enters stud in 1934 at Widener's Erdenheim Farm near Philadelphia. In 1935, he relocates to Widener's Old Kenney Farm, partitioned from his uncle Joe Widener's historic Elmendorf Farm outside of Lexington. Jamestown will sire 1939 Kentucky Derby and Belmont Stakes winner Johnstown. Undaunted, Grandfather never stops recruiting. To Isabel Dodge Sloane, who has just won the 1934 Kentucky Derby with Cavalcade, he writes:

> I have established a breeding farm near Bel Air, Maryland. I have fine stables and wonderful grass, including Bluegrass. Have you ever considered breeding your mares to take advantage of Maryland-bred races? I am in a position to take a few mares and my charge would be $30.00 per month.

There is a magic to reading his letters. A ceremony takes place. I settle into a chair, slip a letter free from its envelope. It opens with a greeting, tells a short story, closes with sincerity. Every letter is a sketch of the horse business. Spontaneous art. Immediate. Drawn in the moment before that moment was lost to time.

CHANNELING HIM

Grandfather rededicates himself to finding a stallion to carry his new farm—and this time succeeds.

The Baltimore News, Jan. 25, 1934:

BUTLER'S CHAMPION QUESTIONNAIRE WILL STAND IN MARYLAND

This state, which is rapidly forging to the front as the center of America's breeding industry, took another step forward today when Adolphe Pons of New York, who recently acquired a farm near Bel Air, announced he had arranged with James Butler, popular Yonkers (N.Y.) sportsman, to stand Questionnaire.

Grocery store tycoon James Butler owned Empire City Race Track in the Bronx. For flat racing back then. These days, it is the Empire City Casino or, if you prefer, Yonkers Raceway, a trotting horse track whose grandstand you see from the New York Thruway, Interstate 87, eight miles north of the George Washington Bridge.

Butler's colt Questionnaire is an outstanding three-year-old of 1930, second-best only to Triple Crown winner Gallant Fox. As a four-year-old, Questionnaire will win the Brooklyn and Metropolitan Handicaps, first-tier fixtures on the racing calendar.

Before computers, breeders memorized pedigrees. Grandfather studied Questionnaire's. The sire line on top: By Metropolitan winner Sting, by Spur, by King James, by 1898 Kentucky Derby winner Plaudit. The mare's side on bottom: Miss Puzzle, granddaughter of Domino.

Say no more. When Grandfather found Domino in a pedigree, it was like finding money. But Country Life's new stallion paddocks are not completed in time for the 1934 breeding season. Questionnaire will stand his first season eight miles away at Inverness Stud, part of the historic ten-thousand-acre agricultural preserve known as My Lady's Manor. At the conclusion of the breeding season, Questionnaire is vanned back from "The Manor" to take up residence at Country Life and prepare for the 1935 season. But Butler dies, and his sons can't wait to unload their old man's horses. I find billing entries for the Butler estate in Grandfather's 1934 Farm Record Book.

```
June 28. Questionnaire arrived from Inverness. Board $60
per mos.
  Aug. 3. Board & Keep 3 days.
```

All in? Vet, vanning, and board? Grandfather records just eighty-four dollars from a deal to stand the rival of Gallant Fox. What a tough way to launch a new farm—losing a stallion he hoped to build around. "Get over it," I think he thinks. Helen Hay Whitney buys Questionnaire for fifteen thousand dollars and relocates him to Greentree Stud in Lexington, where he sires a string of stakes winners: Hash, Requested, Coincidence, Carolyn A., Double Brandy. Questionnaire might have become Maryland's leading sire. He might have carried Country Life through the coming lean years of World War II. I stare at empty income columns for Questionnaire in Grandfather's 1934 ledger. All that effort—the salesmanship, the persuasion, the good fortune to recruit and stand a fashionable stallion—to book eighty-four dollars?

Grandfather never dwelt on what-ifs. He hopped back on cross-country trains to horse sales in Kentucky, to racetracks in Chicago, to farms in California and Texas—his heart racing to keep up. On a 1935 trip to Boston on behalf of Salmon's real estate holdings, he feels light-headed, dizzy. His chest tightens. A warning shot over the bow of his health. Doctors insist he take three months off. He complies, sort of, by traveling to Europe with wife Mary and daughter Marie, where he renews acquaintances in the bloodstock field. He returns to resume the same hectic schedule as before: weekends here at his farm, where he catches his breath, drinks cool farm water, hurries back Monday mornings to Aberdeen, there onto Penn Station.

So immersed am I in Grandfather's life—his letters, telegrams, receipts, photos—that I feel as though I am channeling him, the way parents know their children's thoughts. This is not spontaneous attribution. This is predisposition. He and I are born worriers.

A BRIEF HISTORY OF EVERYTHING

A sheet of thick paper slashed with ink falls out of an ancient checkbook: to blot the pens of the day. A metaphor of sorts. A Rorschach test asking me: "What do you think of when you see these ink patterns?"

"The business of owning a farm," I answer.

The "how much?" The "who to?" The "what for?" This checkbook is nearly one hundred years old, the first one in the history of the oldest

Thoroughbred farm in Maryland. I rub my fingers on blotter-dried ink that recorded the 1933 purchase of the newest Thoroughbred farm in Maryland.

> August 28, 1933
> Check No. 1.
> $17,000 a/c purchase Rockland Farm Bel Air Md.

Less the three thousand dollars in earnest money, this is the first check among thousands and thousands to come over the decades. This is for "The Farm." This is the first day Grandfather owned 101.4-acre Rockland. He immediately incorporated it as Country Life Farm, Inc. In checkbook margins, he distributes one hundred shares; he retains ten, gives seventy to his wife Mary, and ten each to sons Adolphe Jr. and John.

His youngest son Joe is eleven years old the day of Rockland's purchase. His name is absent among Country Life's initial shareholders. I pause in irony that Dad's birthday present could have been a share or two in the new family farm. When Dad returns from World War II to begin his working life, he starts out at ground zero. An inequitable position in which to find oneself, but a familiar one to younger sons—by dint of age, by feudal rules of primogeniture hanging over from the Middle Ages.

Joe Pons begins his working life at Country Life Farm after World War II.

With sons back from the war, Grandfather plans for the day when he is gone. He adjusts the ownership of shares in the farm corporation in the late 1940s, ups Uncle Johnny to sixty shares, plugs Dad in at forty. Majority rule is 51 percent. Dad therefore has no vote that matters—in any matter. When he asks for parity, Uncle Johnny will say, with the air of one who holds all the cards, that a dead-heat in a horse race settles nothing. Family farms break up over inequities. Toiling under an older brother's thumb, disproportionate to merit, with no say, diminishes Dad's sense of self-worth. Lurking in the shadows, the insidious disease of alcoholism senses an opening, begins its destructive work, brings both younger and older brother to their knees.

MANAGEMENT ISSUES

Uncle Johnny was installed as Country Life manager when he was only eighteen years old, fresh out of LaSalle Military Academy on the south shore of Long Island (since absorbed into the New York University system). He wrote farm diary entries in a logbook emblazoned with the title OUR LEADER, a role he relinquished in the 1980s only upon confronting his alcoholism.

In the late 1970s, you could find Uncle Johnny distractedly picking at lunch over early afternoon cocktails at The Red Fox in Bel Air. He sat with pals from the old Harford County days—real estate men, insurance men, tennis partners. If you found him early enough, he would remember that you had asked to speak to him, and that he had set up a time to talk, back at his house, but by that point in the afternoon, there was no sense in meeting.

Four years before he sobered up in 1980, he had sold off five acres of the farm, where Old Joppa intersected with Route 1. The prime corner. Developers were conducting percolation tests on other road-frontage fields on the farm. Easy access a priority for prompt real estate sales. The "next generation" returned home in the early 1980s, bought back three of the sold-off five acres, and halted further perc tests. We rationalized that Uncle Johnny had done what he thought he had to do, like cutting off your thumb to save your hand. In the fog of his war with alcohol, he had wounded the entire family. The healing had begun as soon as we watched backhoe operators fill in their test bores, load their yellow machines onto flatbed trailers, and get the hell out of our fields.

Photographer Aubrey Bodine captures Joe Pons (on tractor) at Country Life, 1965.

There was a time when managing the farm was foremost on Uncle Johnny's mind. His to-do list in the mid-1930s bears uncanny likeness to our present-day duties—excepting the meteoric rise in cost:

> Paid Carpenters helper $12.80. Showed Up.
> Paid 2 painters.
> Lumber $37.50 for stallion barn.
> Start on main house windows.
> Motor broke but everything ok. Will explain.
> Books moved to office.
> Barney sowed field.
> Hartley getting an estimate (cheaper) on fencing.
> Trouble with pump.

This is a side of Uncle Johnny that I have never fully appreciated—what he was like as a young man, a teenager, running the show. Grandfather would arrive from New York City every Friday night on the 9 o'clock train into Aberdeen, and Uncle Johnny would drive him right back to Aberdeen on Monday to catch the 9 a.m. to Penn Station.

Frequent phenomena in the horse business, in all business perhaps, is for aging leaders to tire of the daily chase. Uncle Johnny lost interest, left it to Dad to worry about the minutiae of the farm's operation—what horse goes in which field, what tractor needs fixing, what client needs a call-back. There are photos here in the attic of Dad in his sixties, his arthritic hands on the shanks of unruly weanlings. To be fair, Uncle Johnny would assist in the breeding shed on short-handed Sundays, but his wasn't the phone you dialed at 3 a.m. from the foaling barn. Farm children sense it—parental burnout—and often choose a different career path, away from the land, the needs of animals, the harsh winters, the hot summers, the endless fence boards needing replacement. Family farms fall apart from within as often as from without.

DRUGS, CHEMICALS, CANDY, SODA

Can't you just smell the liniment on Uncle Johnny's 1935 receipts from Richardson's Pharmacy? Knowledgeable chemists at Bel Air's "Prescription Druggists since 1894" fill his saddlebag with a vintage first-aid kit for horses. Who needs bills from an expensive veterinarian if you know what to do with:

Hospital Cotton
1500 Unit Tetanus
2 Rexall Antiseptic Powder
Castile Soap
Turpentine
Blue Stone Solution
Qt. Magnesia
Linseed Oil
1/2 gal. Mineral Oil
2 oz. Wormseed Oil
5 lbs. Calcium Phosp.
2 Dr. Watkins Horse Powder
Iodized salve
Spirits of Ammonia
8 oz. Elix.
Wound Dressing
2 Rubbing Alcohol
2 lbs Epsom Salts
4 oz. Zinc Sulfate
Total: $21.71

Canceled check: paid Dec. 16, 1935. Hats off to horse husbandry—that Uncle Johnny knew what to do with such a list. There's the true horseman in him.

LION OF GOD

No author here in the attic can sleep through my disruptive examinations. Mundane minutiae in the double set of W. H. LaBoyteaux's *Thoroughbred Pedigree Charts, Stakes Winners 1915-1936.* Two table-size tablets, each bound by three steel pins. Like LaBoyteaux is some latter-day Moses, brandishing horse commandments in each arm. I search his scripture for Ariel, Grandfather's first successful stallion, bought for a sale-topping six thousand dollars from a 1930 Rancocas dispersal. Ariel in Hebrew means "lion of God." Ariel was the name of an angel in Milton's *Paradise Lost*, a sprite in Shakespeare's *The Tempest.* Ariel appears in LaBoyteaux's *magnus opus* in volume II, page 541, and again in a 1931 *BloodHorse* story about Xalapa Farm in Kentucky:

> Eternal, of course, is well-known as the shapely brown son of Sweep. Eternal won the Hopeful Stakes, was an extremely fast horse, and is the sire of stakes winner Ariel.

Grandfather's first stallion, a colt named Ariel, foaled in 1925.

Bred in New Jersey in 1925, Ariel won the 1927 Saratoga Special amid Sinclair's legal battles pouring out of the Teapot Dome scandal. Sinclair serves a year behind bars, then disperses his horses. Grandfather sends Ariel to Greenwich Stud (*nee* Nursery Stud) and breeds his best mare Flamante to him in 1933. The resulting foal, Airflame, is born at Colonel Phil T. Chinn's Old Hickory Farm on the Russell Cave Pike near Lexington. *Racing in America* author Hervey picks up the thread:

> Mr. Alfred Vanderbilt had acquired his great stake horse Discovery from Adolphe Pons. Where one has had good luck, he instinctively looks for more, so Mr. Vanderbilt went back to Mr. Pons and secured Airflame, then in his yearling form and a product of Mr. Pons' own stud, in Harford County, Maryland.

On January 8, 1936—officially a two-year-old for a mere eight days—Airflame carries Vanderbilt's red-diamond silks to a debut win at Santa Anita. On January 25, the *Daily Racing Form* reports on his second start:

> A new world's record for three furlongs was established by Airflame, which ran the distance in :33 before 20,000 persons at Santa Anita Park this afternoon.

Airflame featured in book.

On January 26, Uncle Johnny writes in his diary:

Stotler telegraphed from California reserving 6 seasons to Ariel for Vanderbilt. Said congratulations on Airflame's victory.

Ten days later, Grandfather corresponds with his close friend Bud Burmester, a publicist for the Waggoner Family of Fort Worth, Texas. Grandfather had just sold his entire crop of yearlings to the Waggoner brothers, including Airflame's half-brother by Display, the sire of Discovery.

Feb. 4, 1936

My dear Mr. Burmester:

AIRFLAME seems to be the talk of the 2-year-olds. I hope that your Display-Flamante yearling will develop into an even better horse. AIRFLAME will have extreme speed, but I do not know how far he will go.

Airflame is the two-year-old cover-boy of the August 1936 issue of *The Maryland Horse*. Editor Humphrey Finney's introduction:

Vanderbilt's "great stake horse" Discovery at Sagamore.

> The horse that has done most to enhance the glory of our horses of Maryland . . . the first foal raised at Country Life . . . sold privately to Maryland's leading owner, Alfred G. Vanderbilt.

Author John Hervey profiles Airflame in the 1936 volume of *American Race Horses*:

> Trainer J. H. Stotler, managing the stable of Alfred Gwynne Vanderbilt, of Sagamore Farm, has declared that Airflame is the fastest thing that he has ever had charge of.

As a four-year-old, Airflame sets a seven-furlong track record at Saratoga in the American Legion Handicap. Intrigue attends his next start, the Catskill Handicap, where he falters, finishes last, pulls up in distress. Vanderbilt and Stotler suspect foul play and order saliva and urine tests which reveal the presence of morphine. Airflame's groom is suspended. Airflame soldiers on through age seven, but never regains his pre-morphine form.

Airflame, born in Kentucky, but the first foal raised at Country Life.

Stallions are measured by how many stakes winners they sire; the average for the breed is 3 percent. Ariel sired 10 percent stakes winners. His legacy was secured by a mare named Planetoid, the dam of legendary producer Grey Flight, in turn the dam of 1963 Broodmare of the Year Misty Morn, whose sons Bold Lad and Successor both become champion two-year-olds.

Ariel, who died in 1950, was the most valuable horse Grandfather ever owned. Great sentiment attaches to such horses. When they die, their owners die a little with them.

REDEMPTION

Elements of a story: tension, obstacles, arc, resolution. All the ingredients align whenever I think of Uncle Johnny, foregoing college by his commitment to this farm. He would dodge the college question in later life, laughing it away, saying that the Army was his alma mater. I am certain he resented Dad for the good fortune of having attended Notre Dame. This is the stuff of family farms: jealousies, slights, wounds. All fatal, unless forgiven. That is the beauty of all these old letters: their insight, their context.

Long have I harbored an unduly harsh judgment of Uncle Johnny—for his superior air over his younger brother, Dad, for selfish acts as head of the farm partnership, but mostly for carving off the prettiest field on the farm in the 1970s, those precious five acres.

That is until today, when I dove deeper into his diaries from the 1930s, entries pecked out evenings after exhaustive chores. I sped through three months in thirty minutes. He nurses a colicky stallion back to health. He night-watches foaling mares. He drives Grandfather to train stations, off to cultivate clients in Texas, Florida, Kentucky, California. He holds the farm together as World War II looms, and then he's gone for five years in the service. It has taken almost a hundred years for his diaries to find me. It took only one evening of rapt reading for me to begin to let go.

His 1936 diary falls open to the same date as today. It is a Sunday night in a leap year, like tonight. The weather is identical: Clear and cold. It is the night of a new moon—then, now. How little has changed in the cadence of farm life, the rhythm, the flow, in the nine decades since his diaries were written. In three lines, Uncle Johnny mirrors my day—save for stallion names:

Adolphe Pons cultivating clients.

```
February 23, 1936

Sunday
All mares in the barn
Mare and Foal doing nicely
Ladkin and Crack Brigade out all day
```

Among the farm clients he serves in 1936 is Robert L. Gerry, Sr.—powerful New York financier, publisher of the prized book *Matriarchy of the American Turf*, underbidder on Man o' War, member of The Jockey Club. Gerry sends his 1928 Pimlico Futurity winner, High Strung, to stand at brand new Country Life Farm. I feel Uncle Johnny's anxiety.

February 13, 1936

Thursday
Snow and Sleet
High Strung sick last nite, colic and chills
Dr. Gadd here
Temperature at 11 o'clock last night - 102.2
Temperature at 7:30 this morning - 100.2

February 14, 1936

Friday
Rain and Warmer
High Strung seems better today and Temp. is 99.8

His sense of duty. His care of a stallion—the most valuable asset of a breeding farm. His midnight walks to check on High Strung. His rising with urgency first thing in the morning.

January 15, 1936

Wednesday
Rain and Sleet
Crawford's van arrived here last nite, men stayed here
Flanagan's mare Best by Test left for Delhi this morning
Mr. Hewitt of Virginia here to look things over

Insight into who he was before the war years, before the Battle of the Booze. That he saw to the comfort of weary van men. That he supervised the safe loading of a mare for Joe Flanagan—a prominent Maryland racing steward. Best by Test will return here in 1938 for Uncle Johnny to deliver future Hall of Fame steeplechaser Elkridge. Delhi is the upstate New York address of Gerry's Aknusti Farm, where champion Chance Play stands before relocating back to Lexington. Abram Hewitt of Virginia will one day author a treatise on stallions entitled *Sire Lines*, which appeared in serial form in *BloodHorse* when I was a reporter there in the 1970s.

In fairness to Uncle Johnny's legacy, cast in a deserved favorable light, there may not even be a Country Life today had he not watched over his father's farm, lo those nine decades ago.

BOOKIES

Plaster dust flies from power saws as electricians rewire the old Rockland farmhouse. Most unsettling as it settles on Grandfather's books, undisturbed for nine decades on bookshelves in hallways, in living rooms. I peer behind the plaster to see once-white ceramic insulators blackened from a century of use, and thick copper wiring covered in cloth flecked with bits of insulating asphalt, the cloth now frayed and decayed. I sweep my hand across the dust on Uncle Johnny's 1933 farm diary. It falls open at this entry: "Unloaded boxes of books today." Have these books not moved since he wrote that?

I begin my quiet disturbance of the shelves, lowering books into see-through plastic storage bins—the books' spine lines visible, facing out, for easy retrieval. But just because books are old does not mean they are valuable. Find the treasures first. In triplicate, three supple leather covers of James Ben Ali Haggin's 1905 catalog of hundreds of horses on his California ranch. Harry Payne Whitney's 1926 index of his two hundred broodmares, and that of his father, W. C. Whitney, the old man's two hundred mares in a leather-bound book dated 1902.

Here's Belmont's famous mare Beldame, a foal of 1901, in a Nursery Stud catalog. I put my hands on a 1920 letter from Kane imploring Grandfather to get Belmont's permission to destroy the infirm old mare. Kane's letters discourage my urge to romanticize the past.

Drowning in books, I call in an expert appraiser. Upon arrival, Brad Johnson, known as "The Book Guy from Baltimore" among estate auctioneers, appears inured to my excited introductions of Grandfather's collection. For seventy-five dollars an hour, with blank indifference, he snatches down books untouched since 1933.

"I am looking for 'books of antiquity,'" Johnson says flatly, fingers trailing over bound volumes of Dickens, Poe, Hawthorne, Emerson—collections, he says, mass-produced in the late 1800s, and these days "no one wants old brown furniture or old cracked books." Limited editions cause him to pause, as do books with distinctive illustration plates, or arcane subject matter, or author's signatures. He stares at the first of Grandfather's three copies of *Diseases of the Horse*—century-old 1923 editions, replete with Da Vinci–like drawings of elaborate braces for broken-legged horses. I pick up a copy and begin reading to him in windy Victorian prose:

> The poor beast is under sentence of death, and every consideration of interest and of humanity demands an anticipation of nature's evident intent in the quick and easy execution of the sentence.

Johnson shrugs. I set aside all three copies of *Diseases of the Horse* before he euthanizes them.

"Sporting books. Military books. Any of those?" he asks. He consults the web address AbeBooks.com on his cellphone. "Jump ahead to Advanced Search," he hands me his phone. "Drill down by title, author, year of publication. Find out if hardcover, if dust jacket, if first edition, if signed. Anyone can download books from the internet. The complete works of Dickens? Eat lunch, come back, the books are on your phone, on your laptop, on your Kindle. You know they make a wallpaper in that old-book library look?"

He rifles through a hundred books. Sets a baker's dozen on a fireplace bench. Consults AbeBooks on *The History of the Percheron Horse.* Famed workhorse of France. Grandfather stood a Percheron stallion, Sir Don, for a two hundred-dollar stud fee in the 1940s, more than he could get for a Thoroughbred fee. I am partial to Percherons. In the damp foundation rock of the lower hay barn, massive leather Percheron harnesses hang in a decomposing state on thick steel hooks. Percherons: from an area of the Normandy coast known as The Perche. French knights in chainmail armor rode sturdy Percherons in the Middle Ages.

"Do not despair. This book has value. Someone somewhere knows what it is worth—just nobody at AbeBooks. Let me warn you. Do not take any books to a thrift store. They will just pulp them."

Johnson recommends a pal named Russell who operates out of an old gas station he calls "The Book Thing" off Greenmount Avenue in Baltimore. "Russell will not throw them away. He'll resell them for a dollar, but at least he won't pulp them."

Unsorted books pile in pyramids at The Book Thing. Feeling empty and hollow and somewhat in shock, I push books through a doggie door, like I'm abandoning my kids at the orphanage. But the deed is done. I have not left this unpleasant task to others in my family after I'm gone. My sister Norah, well-read, compassionate, says: "Thank you. It's so hard to part with books."

ANOTHER KIND OF BOOK

I am immersed in Dr. E. A. Caslick's 1938 report entitled *The Brood Mare—What the Records Show on Approximately 1000 Individuals at the Claiborne Stud, Paris, Ky.: Breeding Seasons 1932 to 1936.* Mailed to Grandfather eighty years ago and personally signed by Dr. Caslick, "With the Compliments of the Author." The hygienic "Caslick procedure" of suturing shut the upper part of a mare's vulva becomes routine, lowering risk of bacterial infection. Thousands of Thoroughbred foals owe their very existence to Dr. Caslick's "Conclusion No. 18." Prefacing the report, Claiborne owner Arthur B. Hancock, Sr. discusses the 1937 breeding season:

> Sir Gallahad is very valuable. We want to get the greatest results possible. He only made 74 services, and 40 (of 42) mares bred to him became in foal. That is what we are aiming at, to get efficiency, to get as many mares in foal as possible, without working your stallion any harder than you have to.

In the modern Thoroughbred breeding industry, stallions routinely cover books of two hundred mares or more in a four-month breeding season. That's five times the size of a full book in the 1930s. Underreported are the overworked stallions who decide "enough already," lose interest, take hours to cover their mares, frustrate the farm help, find themselves on a boat to Timbuktu. And amnesia attends the breeding industry, the forgotten epidemics of venereal diseases—metritis, arteritis—that shut the game down in the 1970s and again in the 1980s. The gallantry of Claiborne's conservative management of Sir Gallahad is of another day.

WHENCE THE THOROUGHBRED

Saved from The Book Guy's summary judgments: 1882's *An Etymological Dictionary of the English Language.* I open it on a gently pitched lectern, but the doughty old book splits its 140-year-old spine. It comes completely apart when I open it to G. I fix on the word:

> **garret** (n. an attic; a watchtower, from Old French *garite*; a place to look out).

The garret collection grows tall.

This garret looks out over rooftops. Yellow light pours from farm buildings. On a primitive blueprint from the 1930s, the foaling barn is identified as the granary. Other self-evident buildings are identified: hennery, brooder house, corn crib, milk house, cow barn, smoke house, icehouse, horse stable.

I am not sure in what barn the great steeplechase champion Elkridge was born in 1938. But the granary-cum-foaling barn is where the great champion Cigar was born in 1990. Elkridge and Cigar are roommates now in the National Museum of Racing and Hall of Fame in Saratoga Springs, New York.

The steep-pitched, slate-roofed foaling barn is an image out of some Old World fairytale, like a:

fable (n. -Lat. *fabula*, a narration, a story).

The book I am writing in this garret is not a fable, but a narrative exposition, a history lesson informed by a freshly discovered library of papers, books, telegrams—of odd horse-related ephemera—like this pocket-sized, see-through, flip-top Butane cigarette lighter encasing a picture of Carry Back with his jockey Johnny Sellers aboard. Carry Back, the 1961 Kentucky Derby and Preakness winner; not born here but conceived here. Hence, the best-wishes lighter from his owners, "The Prices." Carry Back. Now there's a story that qualifies as a fable.

Hall of Fame steeplechaser Elkridge, foaled at Country Life in 1938.

PSEUDO NAMES

Help me lift this twenty-four-inch-wide, leatherbound *Charts of Successful Sire Lines*, published in London by "Sporting Life" in 1915, written under the pseudonym "Boulanger." Pen names abound in the literature of the Turf. John Hervey was "Salvator." Joe Estes wrote for *BloodHorse* as "Matchem." George F. T. Ryall of *The New Yorker* was "Audax Minor." Neil Newman of the *Daily Racing Form* was "Roamer." I've seen columns by "Exile," but have no idea of the author's real name. Boulanger's identity? He's F. S. Becker, an erudite bloodstock agent. Why the name Boulanger? I find a Franco-Prussian war general of that name, France's "Demagogue on Horseback." That works for me, as equine author Boulanger rabble-rouses the general officers of the General Stud Book:

Foals were given colours which they showed at birth, but no correction made later on . . . if they changed their colour at first moult.

Moult—*le mot juste.* Boulanger uses just the right word to describe how black foals shed into roan weanlings. His *Charts* book is oversized even for a coffee table. August Belmont's signature swirls inside the front cover. He studied this book one hundred years ago, gathering the knowledge of pedigrees that gave the world Man o' War, the greatest Thoroughbred of all time—an arguable distinction among those who witnessed Secretariat's thirty-one-length romp in the 1973 Belmont Stakes.

SARATOGA TRUNK

An acid-stained racing program from 1933 cracks apart at the touch.

27th Day, Saturday, September 2, 1933
The Saratoga Association for the
Improvement of the Breed of Horses

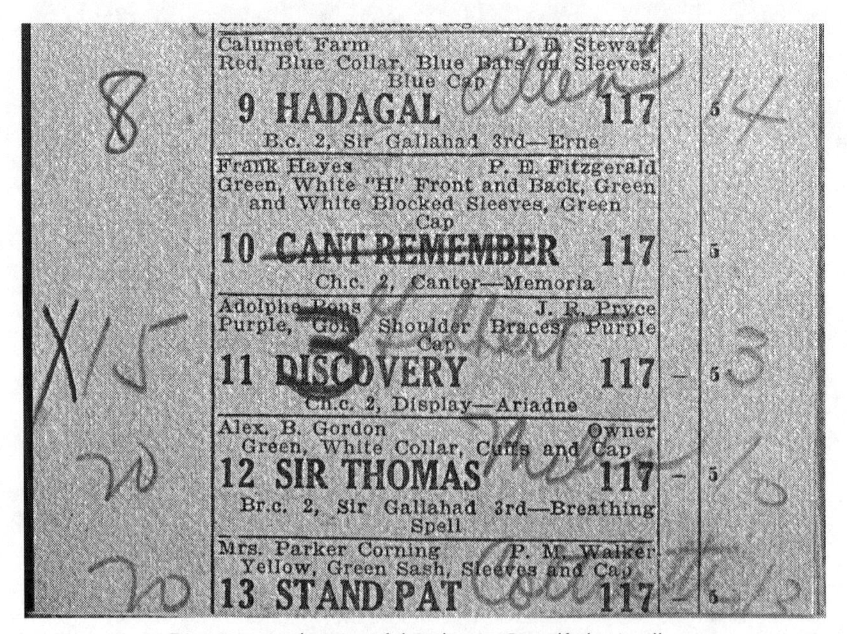

Calumet Farm D. B. Stewart
Red, Blue Collar, Blue Bars on Sleeves, Blue Cap
9 HADAGAL 117 — 5
B.c. 2, Sir Gallahad 3rd—Erne

Frank Hayes P. E. Fitzgerald
Green, White "H" Front and Back, Green and White Blocked Sleeves, Green Cap
10 ~~CANT REMEMBER~~ 117 — 5
Ch.c. 2, Canter—Memoria

Adolphe Pons J. R. Pryce
Purple, Gold Shoulder Braces, Purple Cap
11 DISCOVERY 117 — 5
Ch.c. 2, Display—Ariadne

Alex. B. Gordon Owner
Green, White Collar, Cuffs and Cap
12 SIR THOMAS 117 — 5
Br.c. 2, Sir Gallahad 3rd—Breathing Spell

Mrs. Parker Corning P. M. Walker
Yellow, Green Sash, Sleeves and Cap
13 STAND PAT 117 — 5

Discovery in the Hopeful Stakes in Grandfather's silks.

It is the afternoon of the best-named race ever: The Hopeful Stakes. I meet Grandfather sitting in a wicker chair under a red awning. He is busy penciling in the odds, the jockeys, the orders of finish. He makes a single bright mark in red ink, an X next to DISCOVERY.

```
Owner Adolphe Pons
Purple, Gold Shoulder Braces, Purple Cap
Trainer J. R. Pryce
Ch. c. 2, by Display—Ariadne
```

I pause at the name Ariadne. Feels Greek to me. For distinctive horse names, owners often mine classic literature, or dive into Greek mythology, or crack open the family Bible. Ariadne was a goddess who gave a ball of magic twine to her lover for him to escape a labyrinth. Who knew? How does a horse name in a brittle program from the day of the 1933 Hopeful Stakes trip me into such minutiae? Look around this room: encyclopedias everywhere, and Bibles and missals, and the Oxford English Dictionary (the "OED" in lexicographer lingo), and Webster's Writing Companion handbooks, and books on the law, and Rules of Racing books. The library gods are insistent: If you don't know something, *look it up*.

Discovery runs in Grandfather's purple-and-gold silks in the second year of his lease of the Mereworth Stud racing stable of Walter J. Salmon. A crafty New York City commercial landlord, Salmon is sheltering his equine assets from Depression-era creditors. He offers a self-interested carrot to Grandfather, in essence this deal:

"I get the first $100,000 in purse money. You get ten percent of any earnings above that."

In 1932, the first year of this ambitious arrangement, Grandfather campaigns Mereworth-bred two-year-old filly Swivel. She is a daughter of Mereworth stallion Display, a son of Fair Play and winner of the 1925 Preakness Stakes. Bigger and faster than her counterpart colts, Swivel beats the boys in the one-hundred-thousand-dollar Pimlico Futurity. It is the richest race of the year in the entire country. The winner's share is sixty thousand dollars, credited to Salmon, as per the lease agreement, but that sum sends Grandfather over the one-hundred-thousand-dollar threshold. His 10 percent commission now kicks in.

The very next year, continuing the lease, Grandfather races two-year-old Discovery in his silks thirteen times before the colt is sold. In the Hopeful Stakes, Discovery faces an overflowing field of fourteen other two-year-olds.

Colonel E. R. Bradley wins with Bazaar. Isabel Dodge Sloane's Brookmeade Farm runs second with High Quest (winner of next year's Preakness). Discovery is a good third. The top three finishers share the Hopeful purse of $35,480. Grandfather is once again clawing his way up to the one-hundred-thousand-dollar mark. Within days of the Hopeful Stakes, with the winds of fortune in his favor, he signs the papers to buy Rockland. A good horse makes you feel expansive.

CAPITAL D

Neither Belmont I nor II owned the land under the historic Nursery Stud. They leased it. In 1925, Grandfather assumes the Belmont lease. He takes on a partner, William B. Miller, chairman of the Norwalk Rubber and Tire Company of Greenwich, Connecticut. They do business as Greenwich Stud, retain farm manager Elizabeth Kane and all her staff. Grandfather pays ten thousand dollars a year (twenty-five hundred dollars quarterly) to lease the 339 acres from the estate of Mary Louisa Sutton Norton, late of Washington, DC, and her daughter Juliet May Johnson. The Suttons are an old Southern family from Georgetown, Kentucky; Miller is a Northeast neophyte in the world of horse farming.

May 24, 1926

Mr. Adolphe Pons
C/o August Belmont & Co.,
45 Cedar Street
New York, N.Y.

Dear Mr. Pons:

I have just had a shock as I received the results of the survey of the farm to find that there are 280 acres available. I understood them to say there were 400 acres.

The Norton Estate are receiving on a basis of 300 acres at approximately $20.00 per acre per year, and I consider them well paid, considering that there has never been any investment by them in fencing or buildings.

Yours very truly,
W. B. Miller

Grandfather orders a civil engineer to prepare an aerial view on blueprint paper, a "Block Plan." Sheds, ponds, barns, homes. Stone fence on the Coldstream Farm border. Swinging gate on the Georgetown Pike. Grandfather pencils the precise acreage: 339.104. Miller is not being overcharged by the Norton estate. He is just new to the never-ending expenses, the everyday surprises, of running a horse farm.

Sept. 19, 1927

My dear Mr. Miller:

I enclose you herewith a list of the cost of oats, hay, and straw, month by month. There is not such a great difference in the price of oats, but the price of hay and straw is very striking.

Straw has doubled in price.

It was Major Belmont's custom to purchase his year's supply of hay and straw at harvest time when prices were lowest. We generally put in 100 tons of straw and 200 tons of hay.

I also enclose you a list of horses at the Nursery for four years. Hoping these will help you making satisfactory comparison.

Sincerely,
Adolphe Pons

In this loft of letters, Grandfather speaks out of the Great Depression.

Mr. Bruce Baird
Trust Officer, National Savings and Trust Company
Washington, D.C.

Dear Mr. Baird:

Mr. Miller has just returned from Lexington, where he attended the November sales. He sold nine horses for a total of $1,800. I sold nine at Timonium for $2,020. So, you can see the horse market is shot to pieces.

Paul Johnson, lawyer for the Norton estate:

We are quite aware of conditions.

Grandfather back to Johnson:

Farms at the present time in Kentucky are being offered at half of the former rentals. I cannot do the impossible. I am at a loss to know what to do.

Harried, agitated, Grandfather is shaken. How many horse farmers through time have felt this same dread at changes in the market? When he writes "I am at a loss," my heart hurts for him, and I think of a line in the novel *All the Light We Cannot See*, Anthony Doerr's account of a Frenchman living under German occupation during World War II:

"As though some beast breathes all the time at the windowpanes of his mind."

I stare through the windowpanes of the garret. I understand now why so many safety deposit boxes up here were empty: their contents had been liquidated or rendered worthless. John Hervey in *Racing in America 1922–1936* titles a chapter:

Third Period: 1930–1933

In terse italicized marginalia:

The Drop in Values of Blood Stock
Drought in Kentucky and Virginia
Stakes and Purses Shrink
Difficult Breeding Conditions

Grandfather pleads for understanding from lawyer Johnson.

In the interest of the Estate of Mary Louisa Norton, you should take into consideration the present depression.

History will soon capitalize the "d" in this great depression.

ON FIRST LOOKING

Through wavy windows, I see the farm below. First time this spring we have left the oldest foals out all night. How pleasing a distraction for late-evening commuters on Route 1—on their crawling, halting, exhausting drives home from the city. The symmetry of handsome four-board fencing such a relief from the sight of strip malls. Fourteen foals at play beside fourteen dams, at sunset, in shades of red. Ah, but with one startled snort, away they go, all twenty-eight horses. An evening treat for drivers, the spectacle of a herd of galloping horses, a hundred-some hooves pounding.

Poet John Keats, on reading a fresh translation of Homer's poetry, wrote a sonnet about newfound appreciation: "On First Looking into Chapman's Homer." How many commuters, new neighbors in the hundreds of apartments across Route 1, are first looking into these fields, with newfound appreciation for horses and for the farms the horses live on?

Broodmares rear up, race down the hill, dazzle their out-of-breath foals. The worrier in me asks: "What if they can't stop?" Nothing good was ever created out of worry, so I turn back into the room and imagine Grandfather, on first looking into his Country Life fields distant evenings past. He had just spent a fortune on board fences, on locust posts. In the spring of 1934, he writes:

> Tell the van driver that my place is two miles before you reach Bel Air, on Route No. 1. He can see the new fences.

New fencing or not, injuries occur. Imagine his regret informing Mr. W. T. Payne, of New York City, this news:

> Yesterday afternoon we had a terrific thunderstorm which started all the mares to run in the fields. PORTERETTE, always active and flighty, ran into the fence, tore her right hind leg very badly. Our veterinarian gave her tetanus antitoxin and sewed and treated her leg. Please notify your insurance company at once. I assure you this accident was unavoidable. We are doing all we can to pull her through.

WARRIORS

Archives rest on makeshift sawhorse tables, waist high, like gurneys, like stretchers. Awaiting examination is the file of Lieutenant Colonel John P. Pons of the US Army Remount, a branch of the cavalry started by General U. S. Grant during the Civil War. Uncle Johnny begins his military career in Virginia at the Quartermaster Depot in Front Royal, and ends it in remote Oklahoma, at Fort Reno, on the Southern Plains, on Cheyenne and Arapaho land, scene of Indian Wars. He serves fifty-four months—a 4 1/2-year absence from Country Life, from his role as aide-de-camp to his father. I follow his career by examining envelopes stamped:

War Department Special Order No. 152:
To deliver shipment of German Prisoners of War.

Thousands of German soldiers of the defeated Afrika Corps arrive at Fort Reno. They build chapels, barracks, officers' quarters. A second wave of prisoners of war (POWs) arrive after the Allied invasion of France. Fort Reno was one in a network of military bases in God-forsaken country where POWs attempting escape could easily be tracked by attack dogs. Official reports use the word "disturbances" as a catch-all for serious incidents: death from lingering war wounds, from suicide or disease, from botched escape attempts. I read the names of forty-six POWs who died at Fort Reno, German boys interred alongside American boys in the military cemetery. I scan lists of captured soldiers arriving by train.

Transfer List No. 2, July 1, 1945: Otto Geisert, Karl Kaiser, Ernst Ihm, Hans Loof, Heinrich Reinecke, Xaver Zeller . . .

Otto, Karl, Ernst, Hans, Heinrich, Xaver. What had they seen of the horrors of war? Post-traumatic stress disorder was not yet a diagnosis. They called it battle fatigue, or shellshock. Irreparable damage to the psyche.

Watch your back, Uncle Johnny. Don't go down in the books as the victim of just another "disturbance."

Uncle Johnny owned his own horse in the Remount: Sager Angel. How thorough the records are for even a horse in wartime.

Report of Annual Inspection of Private Mount

Name: Sager Angel
Color: Chestnut Gelding
Height: 16-2
Weight: 1,160
Breed: 7/8TB
Sire: Chilhowee
Dam: Bad Angel
Foaled: 4/23/38 at Front Royal
Peculiar marks, brands, etc.: Star and trace, 1/2 stk'g LH

Everything connects in the garret. Sager Angel's sire is Chilhowee, a Thoroughbred stallion Grandfather managed for George H. Sloane of Brookmeade Stable. I find Chilhowee's 1920s promotional brochures in Sloane's file. Chilhowee, a Cherokee name. Ironic that he will someday stand at stud in forts from the Indian Wars.

EXCEPTIONAL FARM HANDS

The Aegis
February 15, 1946

100 PRISONERS AVAILABLE FOR WORK

Starting Tuesday, February 12th and continuing until May 1st, 100 prisoners of war at Edgewood Arsenal have been made available for farm work. With very few exceptions, the POWs have proved satisfactory workers.

Exceptions? Could you please be more specific? I'm left to consider the mindset of enemy soldiers—their anger at being captured, at being defeated. But what do I know? Maybe they were glad to be done with the awful business of war. Many POWs, upon repatriation, applied to return to the United States.

Joe Pons at Fort Robinson, 1944.

In the spring of 1946, American armies are still mustering out. Dad is released from active duty at Fort Robinson in northwest Nebraska, the fort where Crazy Horse turned himself in and ended the Great Sioux War. Dad hops in a Jeep bound for Denver, Colorado, with his war buddies to celebrate in the Ship Tavern of the Brown Palace Hotel. Uncle Johnny remains at Fort Reno filling out prisoner paperwork. No relief for exhausted Grandfather. He drives six miles to the Edgewood Arsenal and back twice a day, ferrying POWs. The record is silent whether he encountered any hard cases, any of the very few "exceptions." But how could he not have?

Two years after the war. Local boys returning. Farms recovering. Racing in America is thriving; new stallions are arriving. A 1948 front-page photo from *The Aegis* of Grandfather's latest stallion, with the caption:

> Lochinvar is shown being held by Eugene Fisher, colored, who takes constant care of the valuable horse.

Colored. The way reporters wrote back then. The first true horseman of my youth: Joshua Eugene Fisher, Jr.—sometimes Gene, sometimes Fish, sometimes Josh. I was proud to carry the same name, and he would sing-song this greeting to me:

"Joshaway, how you today?"

A natural horseman. Light touch on a shank. Friendly voice to calm obstreperous stallions. Gene at one time never touched a drink, until one day, when he did. Thereafter, he could not turn one down. In time, it killed him. In a small wooden house on the farm, his eight children were born. Not in a hospital—but right here, on this farm. Their mother Hester helped raise us. To cross Hester was to risk corporal punishment. One day Gene and Hester and their eight children vanished from the farm. I'm certain his drinking played the major part. Hester returned decades later to help us raise our children, without the wooden spoon of her first tour of duty.

Gene on the front page of *The Aegis* triggered such recall. Everywhere I look in this attic of archives are such papers. I think of a sentence from Ernest Hemingway's *A Natural History of the Dead.* He writes: "The surprising thing is the amount of paper scattered about."

THEMES

An afternoon storm clips through, slapping rain on wind-blown fields. The grass greens up before your eyes. Wind out of the South. Warped horn note of Amtrak's Northeast Regional five miles downstream whines up the Winters Run watershed. I walk past clusters of pregnant mares, hind-quarters to the wind. Three here. Two there. A dozen? The mares graze and walk, graze and walk. Never pausing long. Defense measure? Fear of being prey? Eating light in case of flight? I speak to them in assuring tones, because horses like it, and because Cormac McCarthy wrote that a horse thinks if you are talking, you can't be busy tricking him.

Wood ducks splash onto the pond. A Great Blue Heron telescopes his long neck into his chest, thinks he's invisible. Tundra swans hoot on high; after their strand of white wings fades, their song still plays on the wind. Imprinted in spring mud, a set of large, webbed feet. Unfamiliar tracks. But whose? On a rushed drive to the foaling barn last week, I felt a bump under the car. On my way back, I saw that I had run over a beaver. That's whose. Deer stare from the cover of trees budding with leaves. Walt Whitman wrote that the land, the birds, the sky are not small themes. This is life in the country.

THE GREAT WAR

Curtain of fog between Route 1 and Old Joppa conceals the seven new apartment buildings where once stood the brooding Mansard-roofed mansion of Mount Soma Farm. Shrouded in gray is a sixty-foot-high earthen dam on former hayfields hollowed out, a reservoir filling, to have and to hold Winters Run.

Idled in the mist are menacing axe mowers poised to clear land for yet another new neighbor: a strip mall briefly known as Country Life Village before we rushed to trademark our farm's good name. The developer now calls it Bell Gate Centre. *Why the -re?* In the fog, all that is visible are tawny brown winter pastures, hunter green cedars, black fences darkened by rain as though freshly tarred by ghost workers. I hear the white noise of Winters Run, swollen by rain, its waters splashing loudly over a No Man's Land of boulders. As the fog lifts, earth-moving equipment on the dam resumes the advance, treads rattling tank-like in metal sprockets. A rapid *pop-pop-pop-pop-pop* like Vickers machine guns I had read about in *The Guns of August*, in the Great War.

NOT TO WORRY

A starling flies through an open attic window, flaps against stairwell walls, flies down the sixteen stairs to the second floor, slaps off more windows. Like the clatter of small-arms fire. I pitch open a balcony door and he disappears out onto the farm. A bird in the house is not a good omen. Sense of foreboding as I dig deeper into Grandfather's letters from the 1940s. Hard-wired to work hard, Grandfather will not take his own advice. He writes to his friend Joseph H. (Bud) Stotler, manager of Sagamore Farm for Vanderbilt:

> My dear Mr. Stotler,
> On account of Preakness week, we were so very busy showing people around and having guests that I did not have a chance to see you while you were in the hospital.
> The main thing to ensure a quick comeback is not to worry.
>
> Adolphe

His farm, the world at war, his sons, Grandfather worries about everything. His heart flutters. He writes to his sister Marie: "It is no fun being tired all the time." He is hospitalized. Doctors warn him: "Slow Down."

SUNDAY SCHOOL

An autumn Sunday morning. A bell tower in Bel Air clangs out single chimes to ring out the hour. I stand transfixed on the lane to the pond. In this pause, time loses its grip. As if these grazing mares were here one hundred years ago. As if Grandfather—dressed for church in suit and fedora—were to step out of the barn after morning rounds.

I want to be on time for Sunday school this morning, so I take off running past an ancient stone gatepost, through the yard, up the stairs two at a time. The town bell chimes to nine as I take my seat in class. The lesson begins:

Grandfather comes of age when postal workers stuff mailboxes twice a day, when a letter sent Monday is received Wednesday and answered by return mail Friday. Phone calls are expensive. A canceled two-cent stamp in a desk drawer bears witness to the economy of letters.

Postmark 1941. Grandfather is composing an autobiography for a feature in the *Daily Racing Form*. He chronicles his quarter-century as pri-

Adolphe Pons in the Nursery Stud barn where Man o' War was foaled.

vate secretary to Major August Belmont. He emphasizes the influence of Belmont's bloodlines. He capitalizes all Thoroughbred names. He inserts an asterisk for imported horses—punctuation mandated by The Jockey Club to signal the *possibility* of a duplicated name. He makes note of *ROCK SAND, FAIR PLAY, MAN O' WAR, CHANCE PLAY, CHANCE SHOT. He explains his lease of DISCOVERY, SWIVEL. His writing style reveals him: a cordial man trained to be orderly.

Mr. Nelson Dunstan
Triangle Publication, Inc.
New York City, New York

My dear Nelson:

I was the original owner of ARIEL, for which I paid $6,000 at the dispersal sale of Harry F. Sinclair of Rancocas Stud. Two years later, I sold a one-half interest to Mr. William B.

Miller of Greenwich, Connecticut. Two years ago, we sold a one-half interest to Mereworth Stud, so now ARIEL is owned by a syndicate. Mereworth, one-half; Miller, one-quarter; and Pons, one-quarter.

My photograph is on file with the Racing Form. If you are driving down for the Preakness, please drop in for a meal or a drink.

Adolphe Pons

No hand-me-down oral history can compare. He is clarifying the arc of his life for me, a grandchild he never knew. My wobbly sawhorse desk shakes. I keystroke the word "history" but it appears on my laptop screen as "his story." He is a trusted adviser to giants of the Turf. I find letters from Major Louis A. Beard, a founding member of the Keeneland Association for whom the Beard Course is named. Major Beard manages not only the H. P. Whitney Farm on the Paris Pike just north of Lexington but also Whitney's Brookdale Farm in Red Bank, New Jersey. Whitney breeds 192 stakes winners on these farms. For $225 billed quarterly, Grandfather serves as racing agent for Whitney. Newspaper clippings land in my hand.

Eastern Sportsman Leading Owner of Year in American Racing

H. P. Whitney has again won the coveted honor for the year 1929

The Whitney Stable may closely approach the record of the Rancocas Stable

Whitney's Hall of Fame trainer James Rowe, Sr., who saddled eight Belmont Stakes winners, has just died. His son, James Jr., becomes head trainer. Major Beard explains the coming changes to Grandfather.

November 4, 1929

Dear Mr. Pons:

Since Mr. Rowe's death, Jimmy and I have been endeavoring to reorganize the H. P. Whitney Stable and consolidate it with the business of Brookdale Farm.

We have endeavored to find a man who could do the business agent work of the stable and the farm and represent the stable as agent to The Jockey Club. We have located such a man in Mr. John M. Gaver of Baltimore.

We will be very sorry that the reorganization does not leave you with us. Assuring you of my regret over losing you . . .

Grandfather accepts this disappointing news graciously. He knows a cardinal rule: Always leave the door open. His lesson to me by example:

Nov. 27, 1929

My dear Mr. Pons:

Thank you very much for the trouble you are taking to get John Gaver started right for us. I appreciate it very much indeed and I also appreciate your attitude in the whole matter.

With my very kindest regards always,
Louis A. Beard

Grandfather has left the door open. In gratitude, Major Beard presents him with a complimentary season to Whitney stallion Mad Hatter, 1921 Champion Older Horse, by Fair Play out of a Rock Sand mare, same nick as Man o' War.

THE SMALL THINGS

Most horsemen are afraid to chide their clients. Grandfather did not hesitate. To fellow breeder Will Shea:

April 8, 1940

Dear Mr. Shea:

You have had so much bad luck in the past few years that you have lost all sense of fairness.

What do you expect me to do? Keep your horses without board? Produce race horses without fee? And if and when you sell, we may expect something on account? Is that fair?

Yes, you can get plenty of free seasons, but what have you in produce? Nothing.

I tried to advise you properly and for your own good, but undoubtedly you prefer a lot of bluff.

Don't talk against me because I sent you this letter, but you deserved it.

It's just a hasty note to a difficult client, but Grandfather is so concise that I think of an observation made by author Laura Hillenbrand, biographer of the famous champion Seabiscuit:

> Newspapers and magazines form the mainstay of the historian's diet. But this isn't the way we experience history. It's the small things that illustrate a person, tell why their actions are important.

REAR GUARD ACTION

After the British debacle at Dunkirk in June 1940, breeders become nervous about the international market. Grandfather receives this letter from Ben Squires of the American Bloodstock Agency in mid-December:

> Dear Adolphe:
> I agree with you that all prices on horses now being offered from England or Ireland seem to be too high, and therefore I imagine they expect to win the war very soon. I believe you will see the stock much cheaper later on.

The war they expect to win "very soon" will stretch over four years, and sixteen million Americans will serve in the armed forces, including Grandfather's three sons. In 1940, with war looming, breeders in Maryland pull in their purse strings. Grandfather stands an imported stallion named *Alfred the Great, a son of the great French sire Teddy. His partner is Teddy's breeder, Captain Jefferson Davis Cohn, who also bred leading sires Sir Gallahad III and Bull Dog, full brothers by Teddy. Cohn receives this equivocating update from Grandfather as the breeding season approaches:

> With regard to *ALFRED THE GREAT, his two-year-olds have appeared promising, but do not seem to win. Their owners believe they will make stayers. This is to be seen.

Grandfather identifies the difficulty of launching young stallions:

> There are too many sons of *TEDDY and *SIR GALLAHAD in the stud today, and only a few will make good. In Kentucky there are 7 booking free and in Maryland and Virginia 5 without fee.

He suggests that they donate ★Alfred the Great to the Remount, a popular option for struggling stallions. Captain Cohn types back, tongue-in-cheek, admitting defeat:

> Any news on 'Alfred the 'Little'?

These days, our farm is engaged in a war to recruit mares to our stallions. The local mare owners have gone missing in action, deserting to the camps of commercial Kentucky sires. As the foal crop contracts in the regions outside Kentucky, the Bluegrass foal crop increases. We resign ourselves to phoning up Kentucky farms to book our best mares, while we pivot to offer more racing partnerships. All the while, I feel our back is to the sea—the way Allied soldiers felt at Dunkirk. You want to survive? Get on that boat, soldier.

LONG STORY SHORT

Entire stallion histories—racing career, retirement, Remount donation, even a number-one ranking on the national sire list—assemble sequentially on makeshift sawhorses.

In 1940, Grandfather reluctantly agrees to stand a stallion named Legume, a son of international star Epinard. He does it as a favor to Assistant Secretary of State Breckinridge Long. With Legume comes a draft of Long's broodmares—a big boarding account, an enticing boost to any farm's bottom line. But the Maryland market desires sires who won at classic distances on dirt—not sprinters on grass. Grandfather diplomatically prepares the diplomat Long for the hard road ahead.

> Epinard's sons should produce early speed. It will be very hard to book to a horse of that description.

SNAP! The stallion trap has closed on Grandfather. Breeders balk at signing stallion service contracts. Compounding his error, Grandfather breeds his best mare, a granddaughter of Man o' War named Lady Glory. She will one day be the dam of Raise You, in turn the dam of champion Raise a Native, in turn the sire of the legendary stallion Mr. Prospector. In June of 1942, Lady Glory is barren off three covers to Legume, one of only six mares in his book. Grandfather types to Long:

The Remount Office will send Col. Voorhies to inspect the horse. Too many stallions stand in Maryland for the number of mares, which tends to make a poor booking for nearly all stallions.

The problem with failed stallions is that their expenses breed on. Long wants to leave Legume on Grandfather's doorstep—*gratis*.

Department of State
Washington

July 30, 1942

My dear Mr. Pons:
Yours of the 28th regarding Legume and the refusal by the Remount is at hand. In spite of their criticisms, I had never noticed that he was straight in front or toed out. He is on the small side, but he has virility and ancestry.
If you would like the stallion, I would be very glad to present him.

Very sincerely,
Breckinridge Long

Raise You, bred by Country Life in 1946, dam of champion Raise a Native.

Long is a long-time client of Country Life. I want to ask Grandfather how he felt about Long's State Department refusing Jewish refugees from Nazi Germany, but his letters say nothing. So, I search online, find Treasury Secretary Henry Morgenthau, Jr.'s bitter portrait of Long buried in the papers of the US Holocaust Memorial Museum:

> Long says the door to the oppressed is open but that it "has been carefully screened." What he should have said is "bar-locked and bolted." . . . If men of the philosophy of Long continue in control of immigration administration, we may as well take down that plaque from the Statue of Liberty and black out the "lamp beside the golden door."

Where Grandfather is silent, this attic library is not, providing setup, backstory, context. Speak to the past and it will teach thee.

V-MAIL

In 1945, Father's Day fell on June 17. Same as this year. In that eerie way a library knows what a reader wants, I find wartime letters from Grandfather's oldest son Adolphe, Jr., written from somewhere in Europe. The file opens to a blue mimeographed form giving Grandfather power of attorney, just in case:

> To do any and all acts in my behalf.

Uncle Addie writes on bold red Army stationery stamped as V-MAIL. Censors restrict letters to the front of the page, not both sides.

In 1943. Somewhere in Britain:

> You just can't write a letter over here. You can't say where you are, what you do. Sorry to hear about the gas rationing, the no-racing situation, but that's war for you. Hope Johnny gets his promotion. Glad Joe likes the Army.

In 1944. Somewhere in France:

> What a war this has turned out to be.

In 1945. Just somewhere:

I've been sick. Hope we all don't go to that Pacific deal. It hasn't been a picnic here. *C'est la guerre.*

He signs his name "Ad," or "A. J.," for Adolphe, Jr. It's bum luck to be named Adolphe just as another Adolf has loosed the dogs of war on the world. I pronounce French Adolphe with a soft "a" (as in "affable"), while for the Austrian Adolf Hitler, I pronounce the name with a hard "a" (as in "amoral").

All four of Grandfather's children are in service to the war effort: Eldest sons Addie and John enlisted as officers, courtesy of LaSalle Military Academy credits; youngest son Joe is drafted right out of college; lone daughter Marie is a Red Cross volunteer in Philadelphia, her husband Col. Richard Eddy climbing cliffs in the Allied advance through Italy's mountains. In quiet desperation, Grandfather writes this note to Uncle Johnny:

July 2nd, 1945

My dear John:

I hope you can manage a furlough between July 25th and the beginning of August. It is very important that you come home, as it will be the first time in four years that all you boys would be here, and we must decide for the future of our business, and what policy to follow.

The labor situation has been a real headache. I don't think I want to go through it another year.

Much love, and take care of yourself,

Dad

Veterans of V-MAIL, of veiled communiques, his children know he censors his letters to soften their worry over him, but they also know how to read between the lines. He is saying to them: "Please come home. I cannot do this any longer."

BLACK AND WHITE CHRISTMAS

Namesake son Lieutenant Colonel Adolphe Pons, Jr.: Unofficially missing somewhere in Europe in December of 1943. Grandfather confides in Neil Newman, a well-known Turf writer.

Man o' War's sire Fair Play strides into the roped-off ring at the Nursery Stud dispersal in 1925. Grandfather, directly ahead, clutches catalog in right hand.

December 28th, 1943

My dear Neil:

I had little Christmas spirit. We have not heard from Adolphe since Dec. 3rd and all are terribly worried.

Newman has written to him about a story on Hall of Fame trainer Andrew Joyner. Grandfather replies:

> Well, poor old Joyner had to leave us, as well as Joe Widener, and some damned fools are left. Yes, Joyner first trained for the Belmont boys. It was Joyner that took FAIR PLAY and PRISCILLIAN to England to race.
>
> Yes, the original August Belmont had four sons—which included Raymond, confidentially, who committed suicide.
>
> When August Belmont II died, Widener bought the stock of the Nursery Stud, I mean livestock, for $450,000, then three months later had a dispersal sale that amounted to $670,000, so that Widener retained what he wanted at practically no cost to him.
>
> I bid-in FAIR PLAY for Widener at $100,000.

That dark winter of 1943, Grandfather writes to his Kentucky friend Doug Davis of High Hope Farm—such an appropriate name for a horse farm.

My dear Davis:
The breeding industry is practically dead. Now I have only Airflame. I leased Crack Brigade to a good man near Philadelphia. The yearling situation is really serious, and I doubt they will bring much this year.

Davis is equally despondent:

I will be surprised if I sell any seasons this year as even the people with money are hunting for free seasons. But I will probably get through in some way.

The world fights on. In December 1944, Grandfather writes to the wife of Uncle Johnny's good friend Bud Hackney, a young Maryland horseman who had worked at Country Life before the war.

My dear Bernardine:
As far we know the boys are all well. Adolphe writes that he is terribly busy in France and has not had his clothes off in 10 days. John is now at Advanced Training Center at Camp Lee, Virginia, then goes to Fort Reno, Oklahoma. The veterinary laboratories remain for now at Front Royal, so Joseph is safe for the time being. Marie is in Philadelphia with the Red Cross.
We had a very quiet Christmas as the boys were not home and it was very lonesome. We were not in the holiday mood and did not have the heart to send greetings to anyone. It is awful to get down that way.

A month later, Bernardine sends this:

Wednesday, January 17, 1945

Dear Mr. Pons,
Monday nite I received a telegram. Bud is missing in action since Dec. 22nd in Belgium. Please help me pray for him, that he is alive and safe in a prison camp.

In this attic, in this moment of discovering these letters, the Battle of the Bulge is a trail of tears:

August 18, 1945

Dear Mr. Pons,
The War Dept. has finally informed me of the terrible news which I prayed would never come. Bud was killed in action on December 22nd, and was buried in Foy, Belgium.

Bernardine Hackney

August 27, 1945

My dear Be:
Be brave, darling, as you have your whole life before you. There is nothing else we can say at this moment.

Adolphe

Author Richard Ford says if reading his *own* words don't make him cry, he hasn't worked hard enough for the reader—and he writes fiction. These letters are not fiction. I'm crying just holding them—the blue ink, the signatures, the dreaded dreadful news. That could have been Dad, or Uncle Addie, or Uncle Johnny, or Uncle Dick.

The dark mood in the attic lifts when I stumble across a letter from "White Christmas" crooner Bing Crosby, asking for Grandfather's pedigree advice about mares at his California ranch. A Christmas miracle, this letter, at this moment. I had been setting aside season's greetings from long-gone farms, holiday cards themed with horses, pen-and-inks of stable stars, handwritten notes, wishes for the new year. Amid the confusion of papers, I must have placed another file on top of those collector-items Christmas cards: Lesson One in how to lose a file—set another one of top of it.

"Bing, where are those cards?"

He holds his fingers to his lips, says "shush" as he points to Grandfather at a desk under the eaves, lost in happy thoughts as he writes to Elizabeth Kane about the Christmas of 1946. As though all those novenas, those prayers to our Lady of Lourdes, wooden rosary beads worn smooth by worry, have been answered.

My dear Mrs. Kane,
This is the first time in six years we have the entire family together.

HEARTACHE

To his sister in Marseilles, in whom he confides everything:

August 21st, 1948

Dear Marie Jeanne,

We reached Saratoga at 3 in the morning, we went to the Sales paddock to check on the yearlings, went to Church, it was Sunday morning, was busy all day and went to dinner at 8:30 P.M.

I had a heart attack. I went right out. I found myself in the hospital the next morning.

John sent for Joseph to come right up. I was in the hospital for 10 days.

I escaped this time.

I MUST take care of myself now.

Aff'ly,
Adolphe

In those days before electrocardiograms, before ultrasounds, before blood thinners and statins, before medical marvels that extend life expectancies, he "went right out." How many heart attack victims don't come back? What netherworld did he discover when he went right out? After this episode at Saratoga, Grandfather knows he is a dead man walking—not if, but when.

THE UNDISCOVERED COUNTRY

All alone in the attic, I hear voices. Dad arrives via interior monologue, speaking in my head like the ghost-dad in Shakespeare's *Hamlet* who rides astride castle battlements, channeling into his son's thoughts. A dusty green book is open under one of Dad's old bent-neck college desk lamps: *The Ghost in Hamlet*, inscribed by some long-lost uncle simply "Christmas 1906." I read passages. Hamlet in his "To be or not to be" soliloquy calls death "an undiscovered country" from which no traveler returns, yet here's dear old dead Dad, wisecracking that he skipped Lit class on Shakespeare days.

More jester than king was Dad. He penned more postcards than letters. In the 1950s, a booth in the paddock at Saratoga provided free postage. Under a red awning four hundred miles from home, Dad would write pithy postcards to each of his five children.

"Feed the dogs," on mine.

"What did he say on yours?" we would ask each other, in awe of three-inch by five-inch photos of horses under trees backdropped by the misty Adirondacks, or of horses galloping past the slate-roofed clubhouse on sunrise workouts. Even away on business at the Saratoga sales, Dad was with us. He is still here, a traveler who returns from an undiscovered country simply to keep me laughing. I look for him outside attic windows on the tiny balcony that accents this old farmhouse. I discover him straddling the balustrades, calling out:

"What's the word, sonny boy?"

A SUMMER PLACE

The sounds growing up on Country Life. The bronze bell at the main house tolling across the farm, a slow *claaang claaang*, then a rapid *clang clang clang*—Mom's summons to supper. The bugler on the neighboring Fresh Air Camp sounding "Taps," simple lyrics singing in all our minds: "Day is done, gone the sun."

Forward to today's sounds. The crack of sticks at woods edge betraying a set of fox cubs. The petty quarrels of geese on the pond. The voices of men turning out mares and foals into fields in the half-light of sunset. My work shoes thumping on the forty-two steps to the attic. My shuffling through Grandfather's files like I'm cutting cards, *flip flip flip flip flip*.

Where to begin? Fan the manila folders out in alphabetical order.

```
Estes, Joe
Finney, Humphrey
Harriman, Averell
Hildreth, Sam
Roebling, Joe
Salmon, Walter
Sinclair, Harry
Steele, E. E.
Vanderbilt, Alfred
Walker, George Herbert
Widener, Joseph
Wright, Warren
```

When I say their names out loud, their spirits canter out of the four corners of the garret. "Sound off," I order them. An entire cavalry falls in.

THE NERVE OF STEELE

The E. E. Steele file: 1938–1942. He wouldn't know a life saver from an anchor. Still, he insists on charting his own course in the horse business, and he doesn't want anyone at his Wall Street bank to catch him playing the ponies.

> Dear Pons:
>
> The next time you come to New York, please be sure and ring me up before you come into the bank. Apparently, you are very well known here and your association with horses is equally known and, as I am anxious to remove the impression that I am interested in horses, your visit here will put me in an awful position.
>
> Please do not sulk about it but be intelligent and ring me up and we can always go and have lunch.

Steele is impatient, insulting, patronizing. Inured to such snobbery, Grandfather graciously replies:

> My dear Mr. Steele:
>
> I understand your first paragraph very well. I know just what it is. If I should be in New York this week, I will give you a ring.

Steele disparages the people who take care of his horses, questions every fee charged to his account. He accuses Grandfather's great friend Louie Feustel of billing him for an extra day of board.

> I know you will say "Here goes Mr. Steele again" but I think you will readily agree that in money matters—both by training and instinct—I am most particular.

In plucky reply, Grandfather writes:

> On my books I have the horse left on the 10th and charged accordingly. I really should have charged you plenty for

getting us out of bed at that hour to load your horse. I will give you credit for one day on your next bill. Feustel's bill is correct, and he needs it more than I do. I am sorry to have caused you this annoyance.

A rebuke followed by a concession. Steele is a vice president of Manufacturers Trust Company from where he writes a letter of reference to a fellow banker:

I have had financial dealings with Mr. Pons for a number of years and have always accepted his figures with absolute confidence.

Still, his standard tone is that of entitlement.

As I am writing this, my Discovery filly is being sold. Doubtful she will bring even one month's expenses. She has now cost me $2,500. Seems slight hope of redeeming any of this outlay.

He omits mention of the filly's chronically sore, pin-fired ankles. Grandfather advises him to make a broodmare of the Discovery filly. Discovery mares will one day produce preeminent Thoroughbreds Native Dancer and Bold Ruler. Grandfather reports on the sale of the Discovery filly:

She realized $400. I got Bud Hackney to buy her breeding purposes.

Back and forth they parry. Steele:

I wish racing would be stopped by the government, then the trainers would receive a very good lesson; they are all so damned cocky and so independent.

Grandfather:

You certainly are not very complimentary about all your former trainers. You are a chronic kicker but you do not mean any harm.

Steele:

> I have just had a helluva time trying to arrange for the transfer of this one solitary horse to some other trainer up here. Dubasoff promised to ring me up, but I have heard nothing. McCreery refuses stalls. How in hell will I get to see anything with the new gasoline rationing?

A classic "spoil sport," Steele is too vain to realize that these famous trainers won't give him the time of day. Temperamentally unsuited to risk, he disappears from attic files. The horse business attracts then repels the E. E. Steeles of this world.

BY GEORGE

Formidable face of George Herbert "Bert" Walker, from a photo in Jon Meacham's 2015 book *Destiny and Power.* Walker is the maternal grandfather of the forty-first president of the United States, George Herbert Walker Bush, and he is the subject of chapter 2 in Meacham's biography of President Bush. The chapter is titled "A Real Son of a Bitch." Walker may have been one, but never to Grandfather, with whom he traded horses and letters for twenty-five years.

Six weeks after August Belmont's death in 1924, Bert Walker partners with W. Averell Harriman in Log Cabin Stable. The Harriman family has forgiven Belmont's $225,000 promissory note in exchange for the twenty horses in Belmont's racing stable. No recorded lien was necessary. Repayment was a matter of honor.

Among the Belmont racehorses was Chance Play, a superstar in the Log Cabin Stable. Harriman and Walker see visions of a second Man o' War. Arguments ensue. The partners suffer Log Cabin-fever, a contagion caught by trainer Louie Feustel, who resigns, a regrettable career move because Chance Play will win the 1927 Jockey Club Gold Cup for Log Cabin on his way to Horse of the Year honors. In the dissolution of their racing stable, Harriman gets Chance Play and campaigns him under the name of Arden Farms, and Walker gets the Log Cabin name.

The cordial tone of two decades of letters between Walker and Grandfather suggests to me that Mr. Meacham overplayed his son-of-a-bitch pitch.

BATTLING THE ELEMENTS

Lion's roar of a Nor'easter rattles the windows. Evergreens capsize over driveways. Broken limbs hang in canopies of old trees—"widow makers" say the tree men.

It's Day-Two of a Three-Day Blow. No rain, no snow. Just wind-blown tree-flak spinning like sheared-off propeller blades. The farm crew barks commands over the din of whining chain saws. Diesel tractors growl, plume black smoke, carry thick trunks to an impromptu staging area. Tree men say winds above fifty miles per hour wreak havoc. Well, as Mom would say, it's blowing "like sixty" around here—whatever "like sixty" means.

An ancient sycamore stands sentry in the front yard. Referenced in letters before Rockland became Country Life in 1933. Century-old accounts of children standing up inside the hollow tree. Sycamore: a wood so heavy it does not float. It would crush the porches that wrap around this old house. In the tree I see smooth rings where long limbs have been pruned, and I do not regret the high cost of the recurring maintenance of this farm's stately old trees.

Day-Three: Still no armistice from the enemy wind. All horses in barns. Too spooked to be led in such wild weather. No racing at Laurel because jockeys are light as kites. Sons are home. We take a memorable family outing to Washington, DC. The Potomac River has blown out into the Chesapeake Bay. The riverbed is at its lowest in 130 years. Decades of debris that has tumble-weeded into the dark river reappears. Plastic chairs sit up from the river mud, like some underworld council has just adjourned, secret meeting place exposed. Wild wind carries us to the battened-down stables of the US Park Police Horse Mounted Unit. Seven words where two will do: The Remount.

In the early 1900s, August Belmont crusaded for a ready supply of horses should a great war come. To the Remount, he donated Henry of Navarre, match-race nemesis of Domino. General John Pershing rode a Remount gelding named Kidron into World War I.

In World War II, the Remount headquarters were in Front Royal, Virginia, with outposts scattered across The Plains: Fort Robinson in Nebraska, where Dad served; Fort Reno in Oklahoma, where Uncle Johnny served. A 1942 photo in the garret shows a mile-long Easter Parade of horses down Front Royal's Main Street, led by Major John P. Pons astride Sager Angel, named for Colonel Floyd Sager, head of the veterinary corps, resident veterinarian for famed Claiborne Farm in Kentucky.

John and Joe Pons while stationed at Front Royal, Virginia.

A Civil War cavalryman whose horse was shot would swing up into the saddle of a fresh mount. Hence, the Remount.

Theme of battle takes another form in the garret. A hundred years' war rages in silence. Paper, glue, and ink fight their foes of moisture, light, and air. Letters, books, photos, hidden for a century in dark basement storage, linger opened to attic air. That musty library smell? That's books slowly decomposing. Dampness seeps through attic windows. I pry open vintage gold-lettered safety deposit boxes, sturdy relics from Grandfather's quarter-century employ at the Belmont & Co. banking house. Gold flakes fall onto manila folders browned by age. Keys to the boxes are long lost, locks jimmied by hands before mine. I breathe the dust of decaying papers. Someday, all these ancient records will live in specially designed sturdy cardboard Gaylord archival boxes, magic-marked by year, by subject, by character. Until then, this silent war goes on.

HIGH TIME FOR A LESSON

Clear plastic Sterilite storage boxes now litter the attic. I look for a path through. My twisted sense of metaphor imagines the black floorboards running like train tracks past platforms loaded with the personal effects of dead people. Grandfather awakens, presents me with this morning's station stops.

"Let's start with the incorrigible Colonel Chinn."

Three flights below, the office begins another day in the ninth decade of a family horse farm.

"I'll be down later," I text the office team. "I'm meeting an old client up here this morning."

In Kent Hollingsworth's book *The Kentucky Thoroughbred*, honorary Kentucky Colonel Phil T. Chinn springs out of the Roaring Twenties:

> Chinn was the real article. . . . He had a courtliness which charmed Lillian Russell, entranced customers of yearlings, awed creditors . . .

Chinn's charm wears thin, though, the awe gone by autumn of 1924. He sends a telegram stalling on a draft payable to Grandfather, who replies:

> My dear Col. Chinn:
>
> I instructed the bank to hold the draft to the 20th. You have put me in an awkward position. You told me at Saratoga that your sale was O.K. and furthermore that you would pay me for my filly in cash.
>
> Adolphe Pons

Chinn's farm, Himyar Stud, is named for the sire of Domino, whose headstone reads: "Here lies the fleetest runner the American Turf has ever known." Domino blood flows through Chinn's band of one hundred mares. The sheer scale of Himyar's holdings astounds me.

> My dear Adolphe;
>
> I am enclosing list of 90 of my broodmares, 66 with foal, and 24 barren.
>
> Very truly yours,
> Phil T. Chinn

Grandfather cherry-picks:

> Will you please let me have your best price on Free Love, in foal to High Time?

Chinn appears often in early issues of *BloodHorse*. In reverie I dawdle through string-tied, archived magazines; the earliest were mere black-and-white pamphlets seven inches wide, ten inches tall.

Vol. XIII No. 9
Week Ending June 1, 1929
10 Cents

On the cover is L. S. Sutcliffe's conformation photo of High Time, the leading sire of 1928, from the line of fleet Domino. High Time, sire of brilliant two-year-olds Sarazen, Time Exposure, and High Strung, is intensely inbred: He's 3-by-3-by-2 to Domino.

Bear with me. This is dry stuff, like diagramming sentences. A three-generation horse pedigree contains the names of seven stallions. In High Time's family tree, Domino is three of those seven stallions. Chart it out to untangle it. It's like some equine Darth Vader pedigree from *Star Wars*. To be precise, High Time's great-grandfather is his great-grandfather is his grandfather.

Mental and physical issues attend inbreeding. World War I was started by crazy cousins, the domino effect of too much royal blood. Fertility, that too often suffers. High Time was not, as Grandfather would say, "a sure foal getter."

Domino's presence in Col. Chinn's broodmare band is not enough to save the colonel from bankruptcy after the stock market crash. He does not stay down long. By 1934, he's back at the telegraph office:

HAVE ANOTHER DELIGHTFUL MARE CONQUEST WINNING DAUGHTER OF HIGH TIME IN WONDERFUL SHAPE REGARDS =

High Time's champion son High Strung comes to stand at Country Life. Grandfather's promotional brochure addresses the fertility qualms attendant High Time's sons: "High Strung is a sure foal getter. A real Domino-type. Fee: $200 and return."

All I've done all morning is connect dots in a game of Dominos. I carry the lesson with me out onto the farm. At the stud barn, I play with the pedigree of our stallion Mosler. His father, War Front, is by Danzig. His mother, Gold Vault, is by Arch, out of Aurora, by Danzig. Mosler's grandfather is also his great-great-grandfather. He is inbred 2-by-4 to Danzig, who was by super-sire Northern Dancer, who occasionally fathered subfertile sons. That's what I've been talking about. Just ask Col. Chinn. Inbreeding giveth and taketh away.

AN UNFORGETTABLE JOCKEY

As secretary to The Jockey Club chairman, Grandfather used his influential position to help others—a jockey, in this example.

January 10th, 1922

Eugene Leigh, Esq.
Waldorf Astoria
New York City

Dear Mr. Leigh:

I am writing to you on behalf of Ted Rice. He is very anxious to get a position to ride in France, as it is hard for him to keep down weight. It is our intention to ride him on our two-year-olds this year, but Major Belmont does not want to sign a contract rider.

He is in good standing with The Jockey Club, and I am sure would make a success in France.

Sincerely yours,
Adolphe Pons

Two years later, Beatrice Rice writes to Algernon Daingerfield, assistant secretary of The Jockey Club. Daingerfield forwards this letter to Grandfather, hoping he will persuade Major Belmont to bring the power of The Jockey Club to bear.

March 18th, 1924

My dear Mr. Daingerfield:

As you know, my husband Ted was killed on October 6th, last, while riding Mr. Chas. A. Stoneham's horse McKee.

On the night he was killed, the trainer Mr. A. J. Goldsborough called and told me that there was money coming to Ted and that he would bring it to me. He repeated this promise several times before Ted was buried.

The terms for Ted's contract for Mr. Stoneham were: For the season 1923, beginning June 1st: $400 per month salary for First Call and $1,000 present for each winner.

He rode 7 winners. The total amount due Ted, is, therefore:

6 months salary at $400.00	$2,400.00
7 winners at $1,000.00 each	$7,000.00
	$9,400.00

You can see the injustice of Mess. Goldsborough and Stoneham. Ted has left my children and me practically without any resources. I would come personally but I am greatly handicapped with two infants.

Assuring you of my appreciation,
Beatrice Rice

Daingerfield's sister Elizabeth, manager of Faraway Farms in Kentucky, Man o' War's home, implores Grandfather.

Dear Mr. Pons:
I know you will do all you can in speaking to the Major. Ted gave his life in the performance of duty. Will and can The Jockey Club stand for this?

E. D.

Grandfather hands me a newspaper clipping:

NEW YORK, N.Y., Oct. 8, 1923—JOCKEY TED RICE KILLED AT JAMAICA TRACK; Boy's Skull Fractured When McKee Crashes Into Rail.
Won 1920 Kentucky Derby on Paul Jones.
Rode abroad for several years.
Dead rider's mother and father arrive from Indiana today.
Funeral Tuesday.

It's turned cold in the garret. First feel of fall. Ted Rice died on an October afternoon just like this, ninety-five years ago, leaving bereft parents, a destitute widow, and two babies. Today, Rice made weight, rode through the garret on hundred-year-old letters.

I hit the lights on my way down the stairs. I gently close the door, the last one to leave Ted Rice's wake.

CHRISTMAS SPIRIT

How does this room know what I didn't know I was looking for? How else to understand how a tiny black certificate surfaces among thousands of documents on attic examining tables?

It is three inches wide, five inches tall. It is not a mimeograph. It may have come from a rudimentary copying machine known as a "spirit duplicator." How fitting.

MARYLAND STATE DEPARTMENT OF HEALTH

NAME: Adolphe Adrian Pons

DATE OF BIRTH: Nov. 11, 1883

BIRTHPLACE: France

AGE last birthday: 68

USUAL OCCUPATION (Give kind of work done during most of working life, even if retired): Horse Breeder

KIND OF BUSINESS OR INDUSTRY: Thoroughbred horses

DATE OF DEATH: Dec. 25, 1951

This tireless, ambitious, God-fearing Frenchman is on his way to the undiscovered country. I think of that Emily Dickinson poem:

Because I could not stop for Death -
He kindly stopped for me -
The Carriage held but just Ourselves -
And Immortality.

On reflection, that poem feels too serious for my genial grandfather. Instead, I picture him standing on the front porch, looking down the lane with relief as the black carriage approaches. He winks at me to break the spell, then smiles and says: "My ride's here."

Adolphe Pons's death certificate.

Part 2

PARENTAL DISCRETION

My mother's voice plays in my head. She died on January 1, 2017. I want to ask her how she arranged that. To die on New Year's Day. Like Grandfather, who died on Christmas Day. No wonder holidays spook me, my imagination on the lookout for black carriages coming down farm lanes.

Mom was Mary Jo Pons, maiden name Ryan, imbued with the Irish writing habit. She wore out typewriters in nightly essays on the daily ironies of farm life, letters she composed intermittently, sometimes ten pages long, connecting distant family members—away in the Peace Corps or law school or first jobs. She kept blue-inked carbons, an anthology of farm life boxed neatly for me to find. Humorous, poignant, influenced by writers she admired—Dorothy Parker, James Thurber, E. B. White. Her letters carry an immediacy undimmed by the decades. While on night-watch duty, waiting for a mare to foal in 1981, with this farm on an upswing after Dad and Uncle Johnny both joined Alcoholics Anonymous, she sums up her joy:

> So now The Farm is headed toward dreams your grandfather held and in directions I've dreamed you youngsters would be part of. Makes me think of planting trees and doing things another generation might be rewarded by. There's pride again . . . and hope.

Mom's letters are cathartic, written in fits and starts through thousands of midnights, her thoughts flying fast in her elegant penmanship or in onion-skin carbons embossed by the hard-stroked keys of her Olivetti. Even hasty notes seem gracefully worded, as when she sets up a quick, complimentary response to a reporter's story about "The Farm" in 1967:

Mary Jo Pons (black dress) presents winning julep cup.

Dear Mr. Hagan,

While Country Life lacks hanging baskets of geraniums of the magnificence and magnitude of the Greentree operation, still, we breed and race horses . . . and have done so for three generations. Hence, we do beg to qualify as critics of your work. A tumult of applause for your "Thoroughbred" efforts.

Mary Jo Pons

Sometimes her letters are just questions:

Shouldn't there be a desire to treasure possessions cherished by those whom you've loved? Or should that sort of attitude be dismissed because the objects are really no more than just tables, chairs, faded letters . . . trivia. . . . Which is the right way to feel?

Not till death did she part with Dad, infuriating as he could sometimes be. They were married fifty-five years. He was sober for the last twenty-five of them. He went out in the sudden blaze of a heart attack the morning of October 12, 2005. My sister Alice administered CPR, but Emily Dickinson's black carriage came galloping down the lane anyway, looking for all the world like an ambulance. Dad had ridden out ahead of the dreaded coach. He rides back often. Hangs around on the balcony outside the attic windows. I see him all the time. Just the thought of him makes me laugh.

TO WANT TO KNOW WHY

Inspiration to learn about the past originated with parents who left books invitingly open on the long bench by the fireplace:

Joe Palmer's *This Was Racing*.

The Red Smith Reader.

William H. P. Robertson's *The History of Horse Racing in America*.

The Great Ones, authored by a stable of superb writers for *BloodHorse* and signed by editor Kent Hollingsworth, in town for a Preakness:

To Joe and Mary Jo
Keepers of the good Country Life
May 17, 1971

Mom at the typewriter.

An end-curled Polaroid shows Mom typing a late-night letter in the living room—short hair, boyish in a blue armchair, typewriter loaded with a blue carbon, coffee in a silver pitcher, books on the brown bench. I lean my ear to the plaster walls. Like canyons, the stairwells carry the sound of her typing. Out of *The Red Smith Reader* falls this note: Mom, consoling Smith on the death of the *New York Herald Tribune* in 1966.

My dear Red . . .

Selfishly, I bemoaned this loss and fumed at those responsible for it. I resent being robbed of it. Like losing a kind of dependable Aunt . . . someone who isn't constantly about, yet will always happily appear when summoned.

Summer mornings, if we were lucky enough to be at the beach, I'd buy a pile of papers at the corner store . . . *Baltimore Sun, New York Times, Daily News*, and the *Tribune*. I would walk up close to the water, where the sand was firmest, to sit and read the *Tribune*, to my great delight.

She apologizes that the "P" on her typewriter remains "recalcitrant," even after she "pointedly poked it with my hatpin and furiously cleaned it with a vacuum . . . sometimes 'P's' can be dreadfully frustrating." Smith smiles at her *double entendre*—that she is married to that frustrating "P."

And then I hear Dad pecking away at his temperamental typewriter. Keys thwack sharply off the rubber platen. He is banging out breeding dates for a mare by Lochinvar for the registrar of The Jockey Club. Absorbed in concentration, Dad forgets that his poker club, the Jolly Boys, are in route to the farm. He hastily wraps up his letter. Slaps out four #### and a dozen ************ so rapidly that the black-and-red ribbon slips from its guides. He swears at an absent authoritarian figure:

"Aw, to hell with Herr Brennan."

For forty years, Dad dealt with The Jockey Club registrar, who went simply by the signature: L. Brennan, the "L." a form of gender obfuscation by her bosses at the all-boys Jockey Club. The "L." stood for Lillian, as in Lillian Brennan, who began work at The Jockey Club in 1928 when the foal crop was forty-five hundred. By 1968, when The Jockey Club feted her at a retirement dinner at Toots Shor's Restaurant, L. Brennan's annual foal registrations had risen to twenty-two thousand.

In the following twenty years, the foal crop more than doubled, topping out at 51,296 in 1986. It has since sunk to sixteen thousand as of this writing. (A drop of 70 percent in forty years, mostly felt in regions outside Kentucky, imparts a sense of urgency to this chronicle of letters about the Thoroughbred business.)

L. Brennan's tortuous forms, her predictable "No-Name-For-You" reply to Dad's comical Name Claims, her exacting standards for foal photos to corroborate the snips and stockings drawn in the field by fat-fingered farmers, seem so quaint. Now a veterinarian slips a chip into the neck of a foal, and *voila!* Identified for life. All those sweltering summers of my youth, patiently posing fly-bitten foals for Dad's Polaroid, I never got the sense he knew Herr Brennan was a "her."

Dad's closet compartments contain odd-duck mementoes. I reach blindly into a shelf, feel his poker-chip carousel. It spins on its tiny ball bearings. Dad hears it clatter as he laughs at being discovered: "Nobody here but us Jolly Boys." I find his copy of *The Fireside Book of Horse Racing*, signed by Mom to him, Christmas 1963. I sit on the cold attic floor and read Sherwood Anderson's classic coming-of-age story *I Want to Know Why*—about a horse-crazy kid making his first trip to Saratoga. I am that boy on mornings with Dad at the Bel Air Race Track, in scenes straight out of Anderson's prose.

> Out of the stables they come and the boys are on their backs and it's lovely to be there. You hunch down on top of the fence and itch inside you. Nothing smells better than coffee and manure and bacon frying and pipes being smoked out of doors on a morning like that. It just gets to you, that's what it does.

Bel Air Race Track, 1937.

SPELLBOUND

You find your way through a farm by getting lost in it. You hike through back fields pushing forth spring grass. You rub the foreheads of pregnant mares who waddle past, bellies tight as cider barrels. You slip through a gate to a wooded dell where beneath ancient masonry of a springhouse foundation, a silver stream of icy water sluices through fallen fieldstone, gravity-fed into an eighty-gallon trough. Mineral-rich water the mares drink to make strong-boned foals.

Sharp spring air vibrates with the hum of diesel tractors ferrying hay, straw, feed, down to the broodmare barn, up to the stallion barn. In the farm office, keyboards clack. Someone says "Supermoon tonight," and everybody nods knowingly of the moon's influence on the water-weight in full-term mares—all that amniotic fluid.

I climb to the garret grasping newel posts smoothed by hands of time. The Man o' War crew calls my attention to remind me that the great horse was foaled this month in 1917, on March 29. Then his trainer Louie Feustel hands me a letter he wrote from Samuel D. Riddle's Glen Riddle Farm in Berlin, Maryland, as Man o' War is being let down in preparation for a stallion career in Kentucky:

Newel post smoothed by hands of time.

Jan. 14th, 1921

Dear Pons:

Man o' War is going away Monday and I certainly will miss him. And if S. D. is not real good to me, I am going to tell you right now I am not going to stay with him, as I do not think it will take much for us to have a fight.

Sincerely yours,
Louis Feustel

Feustel feuds with aloof Riddle. He forgets the Golden Rule: them that's got the gold, rule. In 1925, Grandfather persuades Averell Harriman and Bert Walker to hire Feustel as trainer, but hot-tempered Feustel resigns before Chance Play embarks on his Horse of the Year campaign of 1927. I'm in the thrall of history now, awed by the Lexington *Herald* sports section, March 27, 1938, by a photo of imperious "S. D." awkwardly holding Man o' War, with this cutline:

Outstanding turf event in the nation this week will be the party in honor of Man o' War's 21st birthday at Faraway Farm. The public is invited to the party, which will be broadcast over a nation-wide hookup. Festivities start at 5 o'clock.

LEXINGTON, KY., SUNDAY, MARCH 27, 1938 PAGES TWENTY-NINE

Horse Lovers Will Be Focused On Man O' War And His Birthday Par

Event Begins At 5 O'Clock

Public Invited To Attend Celebration

Man O' War And Owner Riddle Await Big Party

DOWN in

Spring In The Air At Keeneland Track

Glenn Triumphs Again

Man O' War birthday headline.

Through garret windows comes the last of the evening sun, slanting over the west end of Country Life, throwing light on a box of unread letters from World War II. The only way to break the spell is to gently push the attic door shut, silencing the voices that hold me so captive.

HAUNTED HOUSE

Spirits shove a frayed cardboard box marked Packard Electrical Division across the black oak floor. When did they stop making Packard cars? Stamped in purple ink: PACKING SLIP INSIDE. I uncouple box flaps sealed shut for eighty years to discover a cache of letters from World War II. Here is the first letter I lift free—from Mrs. Edward Haughton, Sr., an Illinois breeder to whom Grandfather has recently mailed a Stallion Service Certificate.

June 27th, 1944

Dear Mr. Pons:
We received word that Eddie Jr. has been missing since June 10th, somewhere over France. Eddie has been so upset he has not taken time for anything.

Grandfather immediately writes to console Eddie, Sr.

June 30th, 1944

My dear Ed Haughton:
I do hope and pray that you have since heard from him or received some encouraging news. I certainly know how you feel, as Adolphe Jr. is also now in Normandy.
Chins up, Ed. Let us hope for the best.

Adolphe

Fear and uncertainty across the world, and still he boosts a "Chins up, Ed." Grandfather's namesake son is in the fighting in France; son John oversees thousands of German POWs at Fort Reno; son Joe leaves Notre Dame, reports to Fort Robinson in the remote northwest corner of Nebraska. All three sons warily anticipate deployment to the Pacific Theater for the anticipated assault on Japan's beaches, where the lives of soldiers seem so expendable in the great cause. Grandfather's tone turns bitter as writes to Elizabeth Kane in Kentucky about Walter Salmon:

> He has not a single patriotic bone in his body. Only figures on the dollars and cents. Took his son Burton out of college and placed him in the Brewster plant so that he would be exempt by being on defense work.

Grandfather is a frail little Frenchman, giving his all for the country that adopted him when he stepped off the steamship *La Normandie* with his father. And here he is, a father himself, full of worry for his own sons. He soldiers on, his farm falling in around him—no farm ever takes a break from needing maintenance. He files an insurance claim after a hay truck breaks through third-story floorboards when a support beam—a forty-foot vertical pole hand-hewn from a single poplar tree—snaps. (How did Quaker carpenters ever raise a forty-foot beam in the first place? That's four stories high.)

Country Life in the 1940s.

In the 1940s, hay trucks were two-axle utility vehicles. Bales were fifty pounders thrown about by farm help. These days, hay trucks are eighteen-wheelers loaded with dense boulders of Western alfalfa from which the occasional rattlesnake skin falls. Forklifts stack blocks of hay three high. Repairs made in the 1940s will not hold the weights of today. An immediate upgrade is necessary. This fix can't wait. I order fresh oak beams from the local mill to double up original floor joists. Steel Lally columns jack into place. Damn the cost. Get this done, before somebody gets crushed. I've learned there are two ways to read Grandfather's letters: In the abstract, as mere entertainment from a former world, or what they rightly are—cautionary tales.

WARTIME WORKFORCE

Louie Feustel and Grandfather have been friends since youth, Feustel as an exercise rider for Belmont at the Nursery Stud on Long Island, Grandfather as the industrious son of the Belmont's cook. A letter during War World War II is clearly between old pals:

> My dear Louis:
>
> The labor situation is so bad that I have not been able to leave to come up to the races . . . you can see we are just where we started off. As you know, now I have to be the chief cook and bottle washer.
>
> Adolphe

Feustel's son replies:

> Dear Adolphe,
>
> My father and I do not seem able to work things out. I sometimes think he is like some horses. When they are out in front coasting, they are like champions. But when they are caught, give up without a struggle.
>
> He has been on good behavior all winter and looks fine.
>
> Louis, Jr.

Good behavior. Louis, Jr.'s code for: "Dad is on the wagon."

These war years come alive when Coyle Studios develops a fresh batch of found negatives. Here we first see the faces of the wartime workforce. Two teenage boys atop a manure wagon, wooden brake pads on the wooden spoked wheels. The boys pause pitchforking to smile for the camera. A lone rider on a lone yearling in a lonely field. Identities unknown.

Overworked, underaged, unfit to serve in the armed services, these young men once greeted each other at work here, the days they showed up, if they showed up. Grandfather's heart must race in his sudden role as chief cook and bottle washer for this crew. How rapidly he appears to age from his 1930s studio portraits for racing publications to these 1940s photos of life during wartime—those lines in his face, that gray hair in a rapidly receding widow's peak, as though he is fading away with every photo I find in shoeboxes in the attic.

WHISKEY FOR MY MEN

Wartime correspondence reveals patterns of lifetimes to come. Uncle Johnny's letters from Fort Reno ask for cases of Melrose whiskey to be shipped out West—a taste of Eastern hospitality for the Officer's Club. Before being

World War II workforce.

drafted out of Notre Dame in 1942, Dad is suspended for two weeks for "underage drinking." A *minor* offense, he would pun, but certainly not to Grandfather, in receipt of the letter from the dean of students. Whenever I find letters from the 1950s and 1960s in boxes bearing the logos of Michelob beer bottles, or in cracked cardboard cases of Seagram's Seven Crown, eighty-proof, I sense trouble brewing.

Those days, that's how the horse business rolled. These days, the booze boxes portend enrollment in Alcoholics Anonymous for Dad and Uncle Johnny. No family member who suffered through Dad and Uncle Johnny's drinking could have predicted they would both enter AA just weeks apart in the summer of 1980. One hundred proof that hopes were not hopeless. A cavalry of other horsemen followed their lead. Triple Crown trainers. Wayward riders. Kids of alkies. . . .

Try as I might, I cannot forget evenings of my youth when I would hide on the wide landing fifteen steps above the brass footrail of the bar. One floor down, Dad and Uncle Johnny heatedly replayed the day's challenges, that bittersweet bar smell floating up the stairwell.

VANISHING ACT

Not many Turf libraries stock a copy of the *1927 American Racing Manual, Part II, American Race Tracks and Records*. It is a time capsule. I study the names of just a few of the racetracks that have fallen to the wrecking ball: Empire City, Havre de Grace, Jamaica, Lexington, Lincoln Fields, Omaha, Raceland, Washington Park.

My heart breaks at more recent updates: Longacres, Hollywood Park, Arlington Park, Ak-Sar-Ben, Golden Gate Fields, Bowie. Maybe soon to the same doom? Laurel Park. So often, the end is swift. Track owners cash out to developers—most tracks so close to population centers. Laurel is a dozen miles to DC, one of the fastest growing urban areas in America. What if Laurel vanishes? Have you seen Pimlico lately? Most of the grandstand is condemned, hidden behind massive black tarps. No racetracks mean no horse farms. Will this book you are reading someday be like Grandfather's letters? Annals of a former world?

It is not an abstract question to horse farmers in Maryland. This is a crowded little state. A hundred yards from where I sit reading about vanished racetracks, masons coat concrete blocks of the rising Bell Gate Centre on the vanished farm where Charlie Shaw re-erected his training barn from vanished Havre de Grace Race Track—"the Graw" as it was famously called in the movie *The Sting*. We may soon be walking clients through fields of foals on our way to un-Happy Hour at the Bell Gate Tavern. I google satellite images of site plans. Our tiny farm cater-cornered to tiny parking spaces, tiny turn lanes. From thirty thousand feet, this new development appears benign. No noise. No lights. No fumes from fast-food chimneys. But down below, in the path of progress, another swath of Harford County farmland has vanished.

CARRY ME BACK

A decade after their father's death, John and Joe stand the leading sire in the United States—ahead of Claiborne's Nasrullah, Calumet's Bull Lea, Greentree's Tom Fool. Perched astonishingly atop the official 1961 General Sire List is Saggy, an overnight success after a dozen years in stallion obscurity. Yet once before in his career, Saggy had known celebrity: He had defeated Citation in the mud at Havre de Grace in the Chesapeake Trial Stakes, Citation's only loss in his 1948 Triple Crown season.

Saggy: America's Leading Sire July 1961.

In 1961, Saggy is riding the long tail of his spectacular son Carry Back. Winner of the Flamingo Stakes and the Florida Derby before his victories in the Kentucky Derby and the Preakness Stakes, Carry Back is the prohibitive favorite to win the Belmont Stakes and capture the Triple Crown for the first time since Citation—a thirteen-year-drought that will extend for another dozen years, to 1973, to Secretariat's Triple Crown. But alas, Carry Back loses the Belmont.

Saggy advertisement a decade before Carry Back's success.

Saggy, victor over Citation at Havre de Grace.

Carry Back: out of a mare by the name of Joppy who was ruled off Ohio tracks for bad behavior and who was then mated for a four-hundred-dollar fee to Saggy. Carry Back: named for an accounting practice that allowed his owner/trainer Jack Price to deduct his losses years after the fact. How could such an unlikely candidate nearly win the Triple Crown?

I work in a room that contains a hundred years' worth of such Horatio Alger horse stories told in aged-brown letters, press clippings, sire lists, obits, telegrams, V-MAILS, Father's Day poems. Out of the ether of this attic come dreams of the next Carry Back—but only if we carry on.

Carry Back was born on April 16, 1958—not here, but in Florida—because after Joppy was bred to Saggy in the spring of 1957, she carried her Maryland-sired baby in utero to the Sunshine State. Had the Maryland-bred Fund Program existed in the 1950s, Carry Back would have been the most famous racehorse ever foaled in Maryland. Instead, that honor is held by two-time Horse of the Year Cigar, foaled here at Country Life on April 18, 1990. A mere $185 shy of ten million dollars, Cigar's earnings of $9,999,815 rank him as the leading Maryland-bred racehorse of all time.

The Jockey Club long ago decided a uniform birthdate for Thoroughbreds: January 1. Lithe little Carry Back begins his racing career on January 29, 1960, twenty-nine days into his official two-year-old season but almost three months shy of his actual second birthday. He races an astounding twenty-one times as a two-year-old. In year-end championship voting, only Hail to Reason ranks higher.

In 1961, Carry Back almost wins the Triple Crown. In 1962, Price flies him to Europe to run in France's Prix de l'Arc de Triomphe, racing clockwise instead of counterclockwise. He finishes well back. Then in 1963, Carry Back services a book of mares in the spring before returning to the races. The gallant five-year-old horse completes his career with a win in Garden State's 1 1/4-mile Trenton Handicap on November 2, his twenty-first victory in his sixty-first race, before resuming his stallion career at Joe O'Farrell's Ocala Stud. O'Farrell was a Marylander who relocated to Florida in the 1950s, the Ocala area an emerging rival to Kentucky's Bluegrass region. Both O'Farrell and Price encourage Dad to relocate Country Life to Florida. Dad writes back:

> Our house and our heart are in the old Free State. We'll stay and try to bring Maryland racing back. Encouraging results of the Maryland-bred plan so far, possibly to the surprise of many.

Mrs. Katherine Price leads Carry Back and jockey Johnny Sellers into the 1961 Preakness Winner's Circle.

Carry Back's gravestone near the Kentucky Derby Museum carries his nickname: "The People's Horse." I was six years old when he won the Derby. Mom sternly shushed her brood of five children, ages three to nine, as we watched on television. We strained to locate tiny Carry Back on the black-and-white set in the living room.

"Quiet! They're in the gate."

Two minutes later, an outbreak of wild excitement as grownups shouted with glee: "He won the Derby! He won the Derby!"

Carry Back is the first racehorse I remember.

APOCRYPHA

Before winning a Pulitzer Prize for his writing in the *New York Times*, Red Smith chronicled racing for the *New York Herald Tribune*. Before the Derby, Smith regaled readers with the rags-to-riches angle of Carry Back's story. In response, Dad provided cheeky umbrage:

April 19, 1961

Dear Red:

I have been reading with interest your articles. There have been many Aprocryphas re: Saggy. One story infers Price was driving an old trailer to Florida with his three mares, broke down outside our farm, that Saggy strolled over and, how do you say—"serviced them"—and the Oakies headed off for Seminole country.

Perhaps Saggy's name and background don't blend with the popular conception of the Turf's bluebloods, a la Calumet, a la Whitney.

But perhaps Carry Back's story has the appeal of the small man in America having as much chance of success as the rich man, and this theme in breeding and racing has its hold on the public.

Right there, Dad nailed it. The cement that binds all the letters in the garret—that good horses come from anywhere. Two unlikely Hall of Famers came from right here. Carry Back, carried away from Country Life in utero in a trailer from Cleveland, and Cigar, bred for the grass but winner of sixteen straight on the dirt.

I walk home thinking of the good fortune awaiting those who carry on. A hawk watches me from the edge of his woods. An apple tree bursts with buds. Winters Run rolls on to the sea. You would never know life in the country had changed one bit since Carry Back's days. In bed at night, though, I watch the sky glow with the lights of the encroaching world. I know that our life in the country is not in the country anymore.

HELL WEEK

Whims of the horse business drove them to drink. Saggy's fair-weather owner, Stanley Sagner, succumbs to blandishments by New York Yankees owner Larry MacPhail, who owns Glenangus Farm two miles away in Bel Air. Sagner sends Saggy to Glenangus for the 1962 breeding season, then returns him to Country Life by 1963.

The year of Saggy's absence, Dad and Uncle Johnny recruit a new stallion named Divine Comedy from Mrs. Elizabeth Whitney Tippett of Llangollen Farm in Virginia. Divine Comedy's first book of mares in 1963 is full at forty—highwater mark in those days. But beware of self-fulfilling horse names: Divine Comedy is named for Dante's fourteenth-century classic that begins with Easter week in Hell, the Inferno. Walking back from breeding a mare on April 12—yes, Good Friday of 1963—Divine Comedy dies of a heart attack. Kentucky insurance man Ed McGrath foresaw calamity. He knew the colt had a heart murmur. Dad dials Louisville.

"Ed, you asked me to call the moment the horse experienced a change in condition. Well, he just did."

I'm nine years old, standing against the wall in the telephone room. Dad's gallows humor masks his pain. Nothing funny about Divine Comedy's death. No vet to autopsy him on a Holy Day. No renderer's truck to winch him up by his ankles on Easter weekend. His big red body goes into rigor mortis on the grass beside the stud barn. Black eyes. Bared grin. It's a huge loss to the farm. Dad phones a syndicate of the best breeders in Virginia and Maryland. Afterwards, he joins his drinking buddies at the Coachman's Inn in Bel Air.

That Easter week of 1963, Dante's Inferno burns just beyond our front fields. Three-alarm wildfire on the Stancill farm just across Old Joppa. Dad takes me with him.

"It's gotten out of control," Dad says as I hold his hand. "Started behind the State Police firing range on Route 1. A ricocheted bullet, they think."

THE ÆGIS

And The Harford Gazette

Thursday, April 25, 1963

30 Pages

Bel Air, Md.

495 Acres Of Woods, Grass Hit By Fires

Winds And Dry Spell Keep All Firemen In County Busy

Wildfires arrive, Divine Comedy departs.

The fire crowns through twenty-five acres of spring-sapped pine, sucks so much oxygen out of the air that it blows itself out momentarily, then fires right back up. A week later, as I walk through the burnt forest, embers melt the rubber soles of my very cool Jack Purcell sneakers.

RACING IN THE STREET

December 5th, 1933

Little Joe Wiesenfeld Co.
7 South Howard Street
Baltimore, Maryland

Dear Sir:
With regard to the Seabrook Auto-Horse trailer: I do not quite understand what you mean the "The total outside gross cost $135"?

Adolphe Pons

I'm seventeen years old in 1971. The Seabrook single-axle horse trailer rusts away behind the Old Garage. I inflate the trailer's cracked tires, tack new canvas to roof slats, grease the ball hitch. Then I shift a World War II–model Willys Jeep into reverse and hook the trailer to the Jeep's tow ball. I twist the wing bolt releases on the trailer's towering tailgate, and up I walk leading arthritic-backed riding horse Langdon. We are not

Seabrook auto-horse trailer.

one hundred feet onto Old Joppa Road before the Seabrook Auto-Horse Trailer lifts itself off the Jeep's hitch. In my rearview mirror, I see the trailer's tongue spark against the blacktop of Old Joppa a moment before Langdon's face appears out my driver's side window, his eyes wide, look of betrayal.

Locked in his trailer, the old campaigner is racing me and the Willys down Old Joppa—and winning—before the trailer abruptly meets the road bank. Farm workers rush to our rescue. They drop the tailgate like it's a drawbridge. Langdon backs out, stiffly, a charger after a crashing joust.

"What were you thinking?" the men demanded. "This trailer has a registration from the 1940s in it. It hasn't been used since your grandfather's day!"

Sometimes I stare out garret windows toward the site of the ancient accident only to laugh at how far I haven't gotten in life.

TRENTON MAKES, THE WORLD TAKES

Archives migrate from basement to attic in dented steel trunks, A&P grocery bags, glue-gone cardboard boxes. Out of these mixed bags falls a creased paper bearing names and phone numbers of Grandfather's best New York City clients—locales from the 1930s revealed in two-letter prefixes.

For Mrs. Robert L. Gerry? Dial:

BUtterfield 8-0213

BUtterfield 8? Why, that's the name of John O'Hara's 1930s novel-made-movie, Elizabeth Taylor steaming up the set. How can a phone number trigger a sense of place? Because these numbers represented neighborhoods.

There's snobby old E. E. Steele. Don't dare leave a horse-related message at his office in William Woodward's bank:

HAnover 2-7200

To set up lunch with cotton trader Leslie Keiffer? Ring:

PLaza 3-9539

Joe Roebling's on the line:

TRenton 2-7141

Grandfather says to me: "Roebling. A great friend. You'd like him. His family built the Brooklyn Bridge. He stands Case Ace at his farm. He's probably calling to tell me my mare Lady Glory is in foal. 'Why, hello Joe!'"

Roebling's Case Ace appears in a treasure of a book. On rich-red board stock, in elegant gold lettering:

STALLION SERVICE RECORD

W. S. Welsh Printing Co.
Lexington, Ky.
1927

This is the family bible for Grandfather's horses. Birth dates. Deaths. Matings. No computers to prepopulate pedigrees. Every page is filled with his handwriting. Foaling history. Service dates. Most telling? Their fates. First page: Index to Mares.

No. 1: Green Flower
1934 slipped colt by Chance Play
1935 barren

```
1936 barren
1937 barren
1938 Destroyed July
```

Tough world, the 1930s. Green Flower's end is emphasized, with finality, by a slashing red line drawn diagonally across her page.

```
No. 2: Miramint
       By 1906 Epsom Derby winner Spearmint
       sire of Plucky Liege, the dam of Sir Gallahad III
       and Bull Dog
       1932 slipped twins by High Strung
       1934 bay colt by Chance Play (died Apr 20/'34)
```

Better mares bring better luck.

```
No. 24: Lady Glory
        Bought from Preston Burch Aug '36 for subscription
        to Ariel $500
```

Seven of Lady Glory's eleven foals are by Case Ace, among them Raise You, dam of 1963 champion two-year-old Raise a Native, in turn the sire of the prolific Mr. Prospector, who led the General Sire List twice. For having bred the foundation mare Raise You, the name Country Life appears in the family-notes of classic winners, champions, leading sires. A source of pride to this day. An example of Grandfather's perseverance—all those arduous trips towing the Seabrook Auto-Horse Trailer to Trenton in the war years rightly recognized by the gods of horse racing.

FOCUSED

Curled photographs from a summer in the 1940s. Double-exposure of Dad posing a yearling for a conformation photo. He's home after World War II. Shirtless in the heat, he is a lean, single, twenty-something. Dream-like quality to the double image. Two dads stand in front of a four-board fence that appears to be eight boards. In one exposure, he poses the yearling by gentle pressure on a Chifney bit. In the other, he snaps his fingers for the yearling to prick its ears. His four hands still aren't enough to pose the yearling perfectly, a timelessly difficult task. The photo may be publicity for

Two Dads hold two yearlings in one photo.

the Saratoga yearling sale that August. Dad may be holding Lady Glory's daughter Raise You before she heads to upstate New York.

Whenever I write about Dad or Uncle Johnny, my thoughts double-expose. They were both two different people. Before AA. After AA. Writing about a distant grandfather? His letters are always in focus. I learn that by the mid-1930s, he has every stall full on his humming hundred acres. One mile south on Route 1, he buys fifty-eight acres for four thousand dollars from Bob and Bessie Wempe, their 1937 deed describing a right-of-way for the Susquehanna Transmission Company. He buys another thirty acres from the Shanahan family. I find photos of a steep-pitched horse barn like it came out of the French countryside.

Comes the second world war. Racing is suspended. Breeders are frozen with fear. Casting about for income, Grandfather sells the Wempe farm for fourteen thousand dollars and the Shanahan place for six thousand dollars. Today, the Wempe farm is a Texas Roadhouse restaurant, a CVS pharmacy, a Tractor Supply store. High-powered electrical towers cleave the back acres—that utility right-of-way. The Shanahan place is a heavy equipment parking lot, the handsome French-style barn made over into a leaky-oil truck stop. They say you can't stop progress. Today, the intersection of Route 1 and Mountain Road is the longest, most complex stoplight from here to Baltimore. In a 1940s photo of gravel-based Route 1 near these farms, there is not even a STOP sign. All these images jump back and forth in my mind, that overlapping double-exposure feel that comes with knowing what came before.

SOME ASSEMBLY REQUIRED

Bundles of ninety-year-old correspondence. Hole-punched letters secured by rusted brass prongs inserted through their upper left-hand corners. I bend back the brass rabbit ears, flip the letters face up. Exchanges between Grandfather and Manhattan stockbroker George H. Sloane. Cryptic Western Union telegrams, red-lined proofs of stallion advertisements, black negatives of foal certificates, ledger pages of board bills, expense reports, memos on Hotel Lafayette stationery in Kentucky mailed in haste as Grandfather rushed to Lexington's Union Station for the twenty-hour train ride back to his New York office. All this effort between principals, and what's missing? A good farm manager to execute their plans. Grandfather writes to Elizabeth Kane at Greenwich Stud.

April 25th, 1928

My dear Mrs. Kane:
I have a new customer. Mr. George Sloane of the Brookmeade Stable. He is the one that is establishing a stud at Warrenton, Va., and he asked me to look for a good man for him. He must be strictly sober.

Kindest regards,
Adolphe

Brookmeade is the name of the racing stable of Sloane and his wife Isabel Dodge, of Detroit's Dodge Brothers fortune. So ingrained becomes the name "Mrs. Isabel Dodge Sloane" that I had never considered the existence of a Mr. Sloane. Their marriage dissolves. She lives at Brookmeade Farm in Upperville, Virginia. He commutes from New York City to his own farm, Whitehall, twenty-five miles south of Brookmeade. In 1934, she wins the Kentucky Derby with Cavalcade and the Preakness Stakes with High Quest. She completes her Triple Crown trophy collection when Brookmeade's Sword Dancer wins the 1959 Belmont Stakes. He slides into horse history obscurity. He appears to be temperamentally unsuited to the horse business, a chronic complainer.

November 4th, 1930

My dear Mr. Pons:
I had hoped you could run down and spend a Sunday with me. I have a number of problems to discuss, such as:

Harper (he is lazy)
The possibility of interesting Mr. Arthur Hancock in the purchase of the weanlings
The disposal of the rest
Whether to keep the "Stud" Chilhowee here or send to Kentucky
Chilhowee's ad
The time to ship mares to Ky
And a great many more things

Do try and come down here at your earliest opportunity.

With best wishes,
George Sloane

It's that *"Do try"* phrase that gets me, that patrician tone, that whine.

The Brookmeade operation had swept into the sport of racing in 1927 when Brooms won Saratoga's Hopeful Stakes. In the *Racing in America* series, John Hervey fills in backstory:

The victory of Brooms in the Hopeful was a shock. He was the first stake winner of prominence that carried the blue and white of the Brookmeade Stable of Mrs. Dodge Sloane, organized two years before by Mr. George Sloane.

Beginner's Luck ends quickly. Sloane is a magnet for bad news, which Grandfather must tactfully deliver:

January 20th, 1930

MEMO for Mr. George Sloane:

Report re—WHITEHALL FARM
Harper admits the mares getting kicked in the small field was his fault. When he turned them out, he thought the second gate was open and did not take the trouble of finding out.
I do not think he will take anything for granted after this, as his wife is most anxious to have him make good for you.

Adolphe

The flip side of hiring is firing, and Grandfather does Sloane's dirty work for him:

November 18th, 1930

My dear Harper:
Mr. George Sloane has decided to ship CHILHOWEE back to Lexington. He is also going to ship six or seven mares.
Under the circumstances, Mr. Sloane will not require your services after December 31st.
You know I will do the best I can to get you another position.

Sincerely yours,
Adolphe Pons

Every archival letter has a power of its own, but those that are handwritten tremble in my hands. I feel Harper's fear when I touch his scrawling penmanship.

November 27, 1930

My dear Mr. Pons,
Mr. Sloane offered to help me get another job but I am afraid with conditions what they are, it won't be easy.
I know I can count on you to do all you can.
Of course, all this will be worse if I don't get something by the first of the year.

Wallace Harper

Sloane comes along at the wrong time in history. The Great Depression produces more horses for sale than there are buyers. An idea gaining momentum by 1931: the purchase and resale of excess Thoroughbreds to ranchers out West, eliminating those horses from The Jockey Club registry. The movement is called "Curtailment." In *BloodHorse* of January 10, editor Thomas B. Cromwell asks:

Do you favor a meeting of breeders to create a fund for the elimination of undesirable Thoroughbreds from breeding and racing?

Walter S. Payne of Mapleton Farm in Lexington replies:

> We breeders should pay into The Jockey Club $25 . . . of this, $5 being the usual fee for registration, and $20 to go into an elimination fund.

More horsemen throw in their two cents, which may be more than their horses are worth:

> The question of elimination is: Who is going to be the absolute judge as to the qualifications of mares or stallions?

Legendary racecaller Clem McCarthy in his column in *The Morning Telegraph* writes:

> Horse owners won't stand the losing gaff long. As they drop away so will production. In a few years you will hear the cry of a shortage of horses.

Cromwell concludes the back and forth:

> The solution will be worked out under the laws of supply and demand.

Matters move too slowly for Sloane. He refuses to discount his horses. He sends Grandfather to negotiate with Lexington breeder Dr. J. C. Carrick, who immediately balks.

> October 24, 1931
>
> My dear Mr. Pons:
>
> The only way I would take Mr. Sloane's horses now, considering the times and the value of broodmares and the way horses are selling, is to take his mares for one-half of their foals, and at the end of three years the mares are to become my property.
>
> Yours truly,
> J. C. Carrick

Sloane takes umbrage at the brutal valuations. The Carrick deal falls apart. Sloane writes to Grandfather: "I am anxious to see you." How can a stockbroker not know risk? Sloane cries about the unfairness of it all.

Grandfather and I both need a break. Downstairs, I turn on the nightly news to learn that the stock market has fallen eight hundred points today. I immediately climb back up the forty-two steps to the attic to wallow further in how depressing was the Great Depression.

Feb. 23rd, 1932

My dear Al:
I have just received word from Mrs. W. Plunkett Stewart stating that owing to the depression, she would not send any mares to Lexington this year, and therefore would not use her Chance Play service.

Adolphe

Jan. 10th, 1933

My dear Mrs. Kane:
I do not see much use in advertising stallions, as fees will be very few and far between. I have spoken to WBM twice since the 1st and he is very low. He tells me he is going to give away, shoot all animals rather than continue spending money.

From the attic heights, I watch mares and foals grazing away the evening under a cove of trees. Their contentment is contagious. The wind picks up at sunset. The sky fills with migrating geese. A cleansing summer rain wipes away my disagreeable mood.

MIDLIFE CRISIS

Grandfather, as he appears in a C. C. Cook photograph taken in the Belmont Park paddock. Lost in thought. Racing Secretary Victor Schaumberg gesticulates, emphatically, but Grandfather's mind is elsewhere. So perfectly in focus is Cook's camera that I find myself becoming Grandfather. His ambitious genes course through me. If I am him, at that moment, I'm daydreaming of getting away from my grinding life as secretary to a banker/businessman at wit's end to survive financially. I'm thinking of a life in the country, away from New York City. History writers warn about the flaw of "spontaneous attribution." Am I taking liberties with Grandfather's thoughts? But isn't this how history is told? By imagination, based on research?

Adolphe Pons and Belmont Park Racing Secretary Victor Schaumberg.

As I draft these sentences, a summer storm is soaking Grandfather's farm. Here in the attic, I find this letter to his attorney in New York City:

July 27th, 1933

My dear Mr. Phillips:

I enclose you herewith correspondence I have had with the Maryland-Virginia Joint Stock Land Bank regarding a farm located outside of Bel Air, Md., which I spoke to you about yesterday.

Will you kindly look over this matter, so that you can advise me when I see you next week? Thanking you,

Sincerely yours,
Adolphe

One month after this letter, this farm—this force of nature—saves him. It brings him out of his own depression. Three months shy of fifty years old, he has decided to make the boldest of career moves. He gazes up into rich green hillsides of sweet August grass, his first day of his brand new life in the country.

HORSEMAN'S GUIDE

Frightened by the presence of so many Masters of the Turf. Erudite equine professors—well educated, discerning, demanding of me: "Get our stories right." Oh, no. Just my luck. I have been singled out by Humphrey S. Finney, professor emeritus, a verifiable editor-in-fact. He is famously informal, preferring to be called "Finney" instead of all that Mister business.

Finney's autobiography *Fair Exchange: Recollections of a Life With Horses*, published in 1974, was a four-decades-late sequel to his first book, *A Stud Farm Diary*. He had written the diary in 1935 for *BloodHorse*, about life as manager of Maryland's Holly Beach Stud. *A Stud Farm Diary* became a pocket-sized missal carried by every aspiring horseman, prompting the Maryland Horse Breeders Association to hire Finney to launch the ambitious *Maryland Horse* magazine. On a sawhorse desk, up pops a photo of Grandfather standing before the breeders' board. Is he entering this letter into the minutes?

June 3rd, 1937

My dear Finney:

The *Maryland Horse* is now a fixture and has been of great value in the improvement of the Thoroughbred industry in our state.

Adolphe Pons

Finney sips his tea. Swallows a capsule of nitroglycerin to steady his heart. Waits for me to continue speed-reading *Fair Exchange*:

I don't have a very high opinion of so-called nicks. They are generally caused by propinquity more than anything else. More Bull Lea mares were available to Blenheim II because of the ownership of the animals involved; and more Princequillo mares were available to Nasrullah; more Rock Sand mares available to Fair Play.

Dust jacket of *Fair Exchange*. Photo of a horse sale conducted at night under Klieg lights, a Louis B. Mayer movie set, Finney at the podium with auctioneer George Swinebroad. The *Los Angeles Times* reports:

Finney, the No. 1 Thoroughbred auction expert in the world, is a disarming character, right out of Dickens. With his

Charles Laughton accent and manner, he could talk a Salvation Army lassie out of her drum.

Finney's reading glasses slide down his nose: "Eyes forward, son. Go on." I stall for time, look around the room for help. Spot a blue-and-pink sales catalog:

1947 Complete Dispersal
Louis B. Mayer Racing Stable
To Be Sold at the Santa Anita Race Track
7:30 P. M., February 27th

Inside cover:

Fasig-Tipton Company through its representative
Humphrey S. Finney is prepared to
take care of prospective purchasers.

Some old horseman said: "You get one break handed to you in this game, and it determines your career." The Mayer sale is Finney's break. He sells Busher, the leading money-winning filly at the time, for $135,000. She's not even the sales topper, but she's most memorable. Every schoolboy should memorize her pedigree: By Man o' War's Triple Crown–winning son War Admiral, out of La Troienne's daughter Baby League. Breeders for a century will mine this motherlode of La Troienne blood. Headline the next day in *The Morning Telegraph*: "Finney Puts Over Biggest Deal of Career." The Mayer dispersal in 1947 is to Finney what the Belmont dispersal was to Grandfather in 1925: Young horsemen making the most of their big breaks.

"You know that story about Mayer offering Samuel D. Riddle a million dollars for Man o' War?" Finney asks me. Well, I know that Man o' War's groom Will Harbut often entertained visitors with a tale of Riddle refusing a million-dollar offer.

"Actually, Mayer said he'd give a million dollars to have a horse *like* Man o' War. An ambitious assistant made the offer. Mr. Riddle was furious. Mr. Mayer, equally furious, denied flat out that he'd ever made such an offer. But the whole thing got tremendous coverage on radio and in the newspapers."

Grandfather once made a somewhat similar inquiry to Riddle:

February 25th, 1926

My dear Mr. Riddle:
Have you ever thought of disposing of your super-horse MAN O' WAR? One of my clients is very interested, and I think would pay $400,000-to-$500,000—a world's record, as you know.

With kind regards,
Adolphe Pons

Riddle's ready response:

March 9, 1926

Mr. Adolphe Pons
45 Cedar Street
New York, N.Y.

Dear Sir:
You will please note that Man o' War is not for sale at any price.

Yours very truly,
Samuel D. Riddle

HOMEWORK

Mist rises over the watershed. Winters Run runs warmer than the air above. The last unweaned mare babysits a thirsty herd of ten youngsters, nursing all comers indiscriminately. At woods edge, silvery spiderwebs suspend in exquisite pattern—dew-covered, concentric, elastic, a marvel of nature. Orange sky yields to night. The Big Dipper outshines the lights of car lots. I climb to the attic in the ambient glow of auto shops.

My grasp of the past is like the Chesapeake Bay—wide, but not very deep. Learn a little about a little until you know something about something. I snap tops off Sterilite storage boxes, review 1940s issues of *The Thoroughbred Record*. I kneel on the floor cradling boxes of *BloodHorse* like I am some supplicant for the knowledge of legendary editors Joe Estes and Joe Palmer. I unearth magazine covers of the stars of Mayer's racing stable: Busher, 1945 Horse of the Year; Thumbs Up, winner of the 1945 Santa

Anita Handicap. I learn that "The Big 'Cap" was not a standard winter highlight of racing in 1945, but run on June 30, just after the World War II ban on racing was lifted, the first renewal since 1941 of America's richest race. I'm not sure what he means, but Finney's voice calls out to me with pride:

"Well, boy, you're in the war now!"

And then he's gone. I look out attic windows. Horses stand on hills in silhouette against the lights of the car lots. I still feel the energy for some independent study, as in: "Who runs the horse business?" The Jockey Club of August Belmont's day served as supreme arbiter of racing matters—due process be damned. No explanation why they denied Man o' War's jockey Johnny Loftus a license to ride; every year he applies, every year he is denied. That's Loftus atop Man o' War in Franklin Voss's portrait of the champion as a two-year-old in 1919, Saratoga grandstand as backdrop. That's the same year Loftus won the Kentucky Derby, Preakness, and Belmont Stakes on Sir Barton, a decade before the three races were called the Triple Crown.

In the 1930s, Loftus became trainer and manager for Three Cousins Farm in Hydes, Maryland. Three Cousins Farm stood Pompoon, 1936 champion two-year-old colt. Grandfather drove his brand-new Seabrook Auto-Horse Trailer the ten miles from Country Life to Three Cousins shuttling his mares for Pompoon to service. It was Grandfather's boss who banned Loftus. How could Loftus not associate Grandfather with losing the mount on Man o' War?

No such plenary power for The Jockey Club of today. In a match race, it loses out to capitalism. Concerned about inbreeding in the Thoroughbred gene pool, The Jockey Club attempted to limit a stallion's book to 140 mares, a restraint-of-trade issue to Kentucky farms in this age of the two-hundred-mare book. Kentucky legislators threatened to create an entirely separate Thoroughbred registry. No stallion in Maryland history has ever covered 140 mares in a single season, but that does not mean it is an abstract matter. Every breeding farm outside of Kentucky feels the dwindling support of the local mare owners, courted by quota-driven salesmen of Kentucky stallions. The foal crop diminishes by 2 percent annually. The day may come when all that remains of Thoroughbred breeding will be in Kentucky.

When I turn off the lights on a Saturday night, I walk down and out through a house lit by all the development around us. A sudden draft pulls the porch door out of my hands. These are forces out of my control.

FIELD TRIP TO THE LIBRARY

August Belmont II, Grandfather's boss, is the most important figure in the Thoroughbred industry from the moment he becomes chairman of The Jockey Club in 1896 until his death in 1924. His papers were donated by his family to the New York Public Library, where they are guarded by the lions Patience and Fortitude. Another trove of Belmont family records is available to researchers in the Butler Library on the immense courtyard of Columbia University.

From home in the evening, I apply online for New York Public Library cards for myself and for my twenty-something son August. There are fifty-three million books in the New York Public Library system. We only need to see a few, and they are in the Rare Books and Manuscripts Room, to whom I address my inquiry. At dawn, we hop Amtrak's Northeast Regional to New York City at the Aberdeen station Grandfather used so frequently in the 1930s. Five miles into the ride, we whistle past the graveyard of historic Havre de Grace Race Track. With August a captive on the train, I launch into what I consider a fascinating lecture.

"August? Did you know that the man you are named for, August Belmont, was an original investor in the Havre de Grace Race Track when the New York tracks closed around 1910? That crime kingpin Arnold Rothstein also was an investor? That in the spring of 1919, Man o' War trained here for his two-year-old debut? You with me so far?"

The August named for Belmont is asleep. He misses the sun rising over the old barn roofs of the historic track, now a National Guard dumping ground for outdated military vehicles. I want to tell August that Man o' War almost didn't live to see greatness. Instead, I footnote it for him: [1]See Kent Hollingsworth's account in *The Great Ones*:

> Man o' War was shipped to old Havre de Grace in the spring of 1919, caught cold and ran a temperature of 106. The fire of the Fair Plays outburned the fever.

Normal temperature for a Thoroughbred is 100.6 degrees Fahrenheit. Some horses don't survive 105. Hot-blooded Man o' War beats that heat by one degree. He returns to Havre de Grace in 1920 to set a track record in the Potomac Handicap.

The Northeast Regional hurtles past transmission towers lining the Delaware River. They look like steel ballerinas, arms out, dancing on the water. My imagination is overactive on the adrenaline of the trip. We roll through woodlands and wetlands so unspoiled that you can't believe you are this close to New York City. Down into tunnels below the great Hudson River and up into the chaos of Pennsylvania Station. Climb out onto 32nd Street to be swallowed by fast-moving currents of commuters.

"Just head north," I holler to August. "If I lose you, meet me on the library steps."

Ten blocks uptown at 42nd Street, the two stone lions welcome us to the New York Public Library. We flash our Manuscripts Room library cards like we are foreign scholars on fellowships and begin to search for horse references in six sturdy archival boxes of Belmont's papers. Plenty of subway construction documents, but not a horse in sight. Box Six changes everything. I spy a red cover:

CATALOGUE
of the
NURSERY
YEARLINGS

Property of
Major August Belmont

TO BE SOLD AT PUBLIC AUCTION
AT THE
SARATOGA RACE COURSE
Saturday, August 17, 1918
AT ONE O'CLOCK

August 17? Why, that's August's birthday! Is there some line running through the horse universe? Why am I so excited? I am staring at the catalog page for Hip No. 9, studying a penciled note.

S. D. Riddle
$5000–.

This cannot be August Belmont's handwriting. He was a busy major in the Great War. I break the great oaken silence of this famed library, whispering to August: "This could be your great-grandfather's handwriting."

Six small envelopes are buried in the bottom of the box, three of which bear legible names of horses: Golden View, Practical, Priscillian. Then three illegible horse names. I say: "August, we've stumbled onto some of Belmont's horse files." Then we strike it rich—a cache of undeveloped negatives. Racehorses at Belmont Park. Mares and stallions and weanlings at the Nursery Stud. August lifts his head to survey the room. Researchers at adjoining desks sense a discovery.

"What have you found?" the librarian asks us.

"Negatives of Belmont's famous horses," I say in a hushed tone. The librarian comes out from behind his desk, carrying white cotton gloves and a lightbox which he plugs into an outlet recessed into the desktop. I warn him: "I know just enough to be dangerous." I set the first negative on the lightbox surface. Heat immediately begins to curl the delicate film. August pulls the hot box away.

"Yes, you are dangerous," the librarian agrees. He holds the negatives an inch away from the light. Reversed-out images in high contrast leap to life.

"That's Fair Play," I say. "He's the sire of Man o' War." I clearly see the cyst on the stallion's neck that I've noted on his formal conformation photos.

"Oh, my goodness, there's Elizabeth Kane, manager of Belmont's farm." Stylish under a banded felt hat, Kane is wearing a handsome woolen coat that tapers at her waist. Her skirt reaches down to the top of her boots. A collar-pin secures a stock. She wears thin, worn gloves, holds a shank expertly as she stares into the eyes of a broodmare snapped to attention.

"Hey, wait. That's the Major in the same photo, behind the mare—that stocky well-dressed fellow. That's August Belmont." Famous flat-brimmed boater. Cardigan sweater with dark piping. Major August Belmont, in from New York, for an inspection of his exquisite equines. And on we go through magical photos. But who is the photographer? The librarian searches. No name anywhere, thus no copyright issues, the photographer lost to history. A curator quotes me a volume discount of fifty dollars each for his in-house staff to develop the negatives: "Just photo-credit New York Public Library."

It's Finders Keepers in The Big Apple. We hop on the 4:40 back to Aberdeen, August's first trip to New York City never to be forgotten. Two days later, digital images of the lost Belmont photos Dropbox into my desktop computer. I make low-quality copies on an office printer, then arrange forty photos as follows:

- Twelve photos of racehorses against a backdrop of Belmont Park barns.
- Four photos of Kane in her felt hat posing broodmares. In one, she is smiling proudly into the eyes of Mahubah—a post-legged, plain

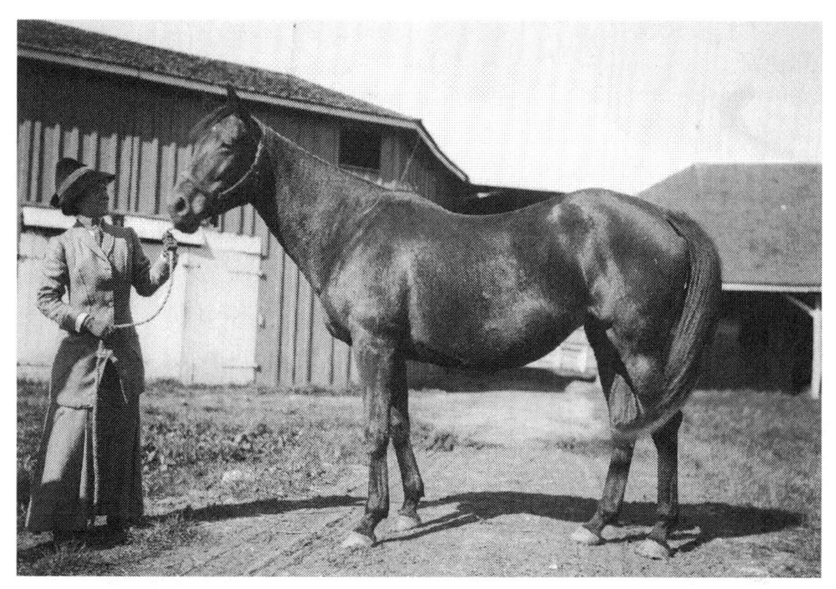

Elizabeth Kane posing Mahubah, the mother of Man o' War.

bay mare whose likeness I identify through reference books and online Man o' War collections.

- Six photos of various broodmares shown by staff.
- Eight photos of stallions, their grooms' eyes fixed on the prized studs. Belmont's stallions descended from the blood of the savage Hastings. They would bite your arm off.
- Four photos of the Belmont broodmare band under oak canopies.
- One photo of four impatient weanlings held steady by four horsemen in rakish woolen caps, in jodhpurs.
- One photo of three yearlings held by twin-looking men in coveralls, Kane's sons Kenneth and Alfred.
- Four photos of weanlings posed by lads in shining leather boots.

All told? Forty photos.

Racehorses with blister paint applied to shins, pepper on bandages. Proud stallions. Mustached men. Dappled dams. Souls back from the dead through the magic of photography, and the care of curates—the librarians. I feel newfound admiration for Kane. All the worry to prepare for a visit by absentee owner Belmont. She's a century ahead of me, but I know the feeling of tidying up a farm for, say, a Preakness Party, or of having horses ready for a client's inspection. How lucky to witness such a day in her life, to identify with her on the level of farm management.

Major Belmont is fraught with worry as he awaits passage of Senate Bill 2083: "To authorize the acquisition and operation by the United States of the Cape Cod Canal." Years of delay ensue as the government moves glacially. The canal debacle takes its toll on Belmont, prompting Kane to confide her fears to Grandfather.

> Nursery Stud
> December 2nd, 1922
>
> Dear Mr. Pons:
> Very sorry to hear that nothing has been done to relieve the Major and his family. It does not seem possible that they should become worried about financial affairs. The government will hold him off as long as possible.

A month later, Grandfather writes to Kane:

> God help us. He looks bad, has grown much older, and looks badly worried.

Kane pours emotion into her return letter:

> March 11, 1923
>
> Dear Mr. Pons:
> I cannot tell you how deeply I feel for the Major. You know that 32 years of association with a person naturally makes you feel like you are one of the family and he has spoken many kind words to me and he really saved my life when he gave me the management of the Nursery.

STALLION TRUTHS

C. W. Anderson composes text to accompany his charcoal drawings of Man o' War for his book *Big Red*, published in 1943. Of the majesty of the then-twenty-six-year-old stallion, Anderson writes:

> The first impression of seeing Man o' War, as he is today, is one of tremendous power. He looks even bigger than the sixteen hands two inches he measures under the standard, and the 1,400-pounds he carries give him a massiveness. . . .

There is nothing coarse about him and his head is very fine, intelligent, and alert.

Anderson describes Man o' War's famous groom Will Harbut:

There has been a tendency among some sports writers to lean too much toward the colored dialect of the popular magazines. The soft slurred accent so characteristic of the Bluegrass is there, but he does not use the double negatives and more tortured grammar often credited to him.

Hours of sketching Man o' War allows Anderson access to a private side of Harbut, who confides to him:

They make Red sway-backed an' me ignorant, an' it ain't fair. Why can't they tell things like they are?

I leap from artist to author on attic shelves when I find Ernest Hemingway's short story "My Old Man," about a jockey, as told by the rider's son.

He'd pull on a rubber shirt and get me to run with him. We'd keep right on running towards the mountains and then my old man would yell "Hey, Joe!" and I'd look back and he'd be sitting under a tree. Then he'd get up and we'd jog along back to the stables.

I've read "My Old Man" once a year since I was that same son, watching a father figuratively battle the weight of the horse business. Out of a Buster Brown shoebox fall photos from the 1950s of Dad holding a menacing stallion, a Hannibal Lecter-muzzle strapped to the horse's halter. It's Lochinvar, a man-eater, the bane of any stud farm. Lochinvar, by Roebling's stallion Case Ace, is named for a knight in a poem by Sir Walter Scott:

"He rode all alone. Dauntless in war, young Lochinvar."

I trace young Lochinvar back in time to the last year of World War II, Grandfather writing to a fellow breeder.

January 3, 1945

What do you think of the racing ban? It is going to hurt breeding in general. And me with my new stallion prospect LOCHINVAR. The ban is killing a real industry.

Savage Stallion Lochinvar.

At stud, his testosterone raging, Lochinvar turns mean. In 1957, at feeding time, he savages Dad. Pins him to the stall floor. Mauls his outstretched hands. Dad gouges Lochinvar's eyes and slides out from underneath the killing stallion and stumbles home across the farm to Mom. He is battered but alive. Horsemen brush off such danger. An occupational hazard with stallions. A job site accident sometimes. Thing is, some of the best Thoroughbred stallions in history have been maulers. Hook 'em up. Muzzle 'em if you have to. Just get that damn mare bred.

I cannot name a job in farming that requires such courage.

ACTUALITIÉS

Coyle Studios digitizes and uploads the developed negatives to my computer. Images I've never seen scroll in a rapidly repeating loop. I think of the very first movies Grandfather saw as a teenager in the 1890s called "Actualitiés." Sped-up animation struck fear in audiences. Moving pictures of waves breaking sent first-time filmgoers stampeding to the exits for fear of drowning.

On and on the photos scroll. Stud men shanking rearing stallions. Stud men posing them for conformation photos in wide-open places on the farm, selected for a pleasing photo background not for handler's safety—on flat driveways in front of wooden-sided station wagons, or in fields unfamiliar to the stallions, who are all about territory, all about protecting their paddocks. And then there's Lochinvar, his head over his stall door, small eyes, unkind eyes—pig eyes in the nomenclature of the Turf. I recreate his attack on Dad, who has turned his back to pour oats into a feed tub. Lochinvar pounces. Dauntless young Lochinvar. The fear Dad felt under Lochinvar's hooves, Dad's hands in the vise of the stallion's teeth. In farm ledgers from those years, stud fees from Lochinvar appear on red-ruled income sheets, as though written in the blood of his handlers. The savage stallion is an actuality of life on a breeding farm.

JUST HORSING AROUND

Authors climb down from shelves. Youthful Joe Palmer, before his renown at the *New York Herald*, hustling Stallion Register pages for *BloodHorse* in polite letters to Grandfather. Grantland Rice. Sherwood Anderson. Damon Runyon. Red Smith. Whitney Tower. Kent Hollingsworth. They tap spent tobacco out of their pipes into their hands. Reload their typewriters. Call out sentence drafts. Thank each other for Christmas cards. Some of their book bindings suffer from what librarians call "red rot." Leather-bound books whose fragile covers dissolve to powder. My curious hands damage these relics further. But what good is a book if it can't be opened?

August Belmont's reference books cooked on Grandfather's telephone room bookshelves through a century of afternoon sun. The life's work of writers became unidentifiable. Just pick a book at random. Good Lord! It's the first of a two-volume set. Titles in all caps: THE AMERICAN STUD BOOK. Entered, according to Act of Congress, in the year 1873, by SANDERS W. BRUCE.

EARLIEST ACCOUNTS OF RACING IN AMERICA
TO THE END OF 1872
ALSO, ALL THE NATIVE MARES AND THEIR PRODUCE

A horse-loving Baltimore bookbinder at Advantage Books quotes me new covers at seventy-five dollars each. To be rebound is to be rediscovered. Bruce's introduction is a 150-year-old lyrical ballad:

> Unless we can trace an ancestral line back to the mists and shadows from which it sprang . . .
>
> None but those who have inquired into the loose, obscure records of the past have any idea of what a Herculean task it has been . . .
>
> Such has been the labor of the life of him who now gives THE AMERICAN STUD BOOK to the world.

On Christmas Day, my two sons, home for the holidays, think I've lost my mind as I exclaim: "The first mare in the American Stud Book is named Abbe Rattler, a foal of 1827. Wouldn't you know? She's a Maryland-bred!"

I brandish the rebound red volume, waving it like the crazy Russian father in Woody Allen's movie *Love and Death* who carries around a clod of sod, telling his son: "I have saved this piece of land for you." Bruce's valuable book slips from my hand, losing its brand new binding like throwing off a winter coat. Mom would have called me a jackass for horsing around with such treasures, and she would have been right.

HEADQUARTERS, NOT HINDQUARTERS

It's only January, but bulbs are poking up, trees budding out. All quiet on the farm. It's the morning after our Stallion Show. A languid post-concert feeling, my ears ringing from the urgent words of yesterday's guest speaker, state Senator J. B. Jennings. Ordinarily, our Stallion Show features a pedigree expert. Not this time. Our beleaguered horse industry needs to focus on the political fronts: local and national. On deck in Annapolis, thirty-five miles from here, is a bill to pump $375 million in bonds to renovate our ancient racing facilities at both Pimlico and Laurel.

"If this racing bill fails in Annapolis, it's over," said Jennings. "The Preakness will move. The tracks will close. All of you need to write letters, make phone calls, show up when asked."

In Washington, DC, fifty-five miles away, hearings begin on "Legislation to Promote the Health and Safety of Racehorses." The idea of unity divides this industry. Each state postures like some tiny Old World European nation—defending fiefdoms of sovereignty, heading for war, led by a mercenary army of lawyers and lobbyists, billing hour by exorbitant hour. When these highly paid professionals pledge allegiance to the cause by saying "We work for you '25/7,'" I wonder what's next. "We work for you eight days a week"? Factotums abound. Executives of horsemen's groups fear replacement by a national governing body.

Open on an attic bookshelf is *The Marx Brothers Scrapbook*. The plot of their 1933 movie *Duck Soup* feels familiar. Groucho, as Rufus T. Firefly, wants to send a telegram from the war. Harpo arrives on a horse, like the Pony Express. Firefly says: "I said give me 'Headquarters, not Hindquarters!'" Then he begins shooting at his own men. Metaphor for the moment. Our horse industry, a circular firing squad. Meanwhile, the foal crop continues its drip-drip-drip descent.

STIMULATION

A 1937 editorial entitled: "Protect Our Horses," by Humphrey S. Finney, as editor of *The Maryland Horse*. Hot topic of the time—legislation making it "a felony to tamper in any manner whatsoever" with a racehorse. This, in response to an age-old backstretch trick: concealing sponges high in a horse's nostrils, which affects breathing, which affects outcome of races.

Today's scourge: Oxygenated blood. Racehorses running the way Lance Armstrong pedaled: tirelessly, undetectably enhanced. Through the magic of the *New York Times* online resource *TimesMachine*, I stumble onto a speech by The Jockey Club Chairman William Woodward from November 19, 1933:

> The evil of stimulation has existed for many years and has been steadily fought by The Jockey Club. Proof of stimulation is most difficult to obtain. It does not come under the head of exact sciences.

Fast-forward ninety years. A day at the races with partners who just lost to a suspiciously successful trainer. They ask me: "How does that guy win so many races?" I want to say: The evil of stimulation affects everyone. But I don't dare say what I think—because then the impression will be that the game is fixed. Instead, I return to the attic, flip to an essay called "Fixing" in a book called *Racing Days*. Brendan Boyd writes:

> It's every newcomer's first question: "Are they fixed?" You fall back on the truth. Some are. And some aren't. There are two ways to fix a race: buy the jockey or hit the horse. You buy the jockey with blandishments, money being the blandishment of choice. You hit the horse through its bloodstream.

CALL AND RESPONSE

The Great Depression lifts. Horse racing flourishes. States approve racetracks everywhere, eager to collect taxes from racing's monopoly on gambling. Fast growth, though, attracts fast money: the criminal element. Reformers take aim at horse racing. In that era, Grandfather's loyal patron Joseph E. Widener is the most influential man in racing. His stern face stares out at me from photos at testimonial dinners, or from Kentucky Derby boxes, or from photos of him atop spiraling marble staircases of his racetrack, the fabulous Hialeah Park in Miami, Florida. Widener is an advocate for clean racing. He introduces the totalizator system of betting at Hialeah. He adopts the French system of random saliva testing of racehorses. He agitates the aloof organization of The Jockey Club as vice chairman. In 1933, Widener is the honored guest of the Thoroughbred Club of America, written about in *BloodHorse* in its issue of November 25 that year.

> Alluding to "the cry for a national board to aid in the control of racing affairs," Mr. Widener called attention to the many difficulties in the laws and the regulations of the controlling agencies in the different states. He offered no encouragement for those who have proposed a Turf organization of national scope and power.

Now, nine decades later, racing has finally established a national organization, its difficult birth predicted by Widener.

I find five telegrams from five days of horse trading in 1934 that reveal Widener to me. He cables a reply from a suite at the Ritz Hotel in Paris.

RADIOGRAM

Via RCA — WORLD WIDE WIRELESS — Via RCA

R.C.A. COMMUNICATIONS, INC.
A RADIO CORPORATION OF AMERICA SUBSIDIARY

RECEIVED AT 64 BROAD STREET, NEW YORK, AT JUL 25 1934 STANDARD TIME

FSEHZ RFK259
PARIS 40 24 2300 LXW 67
NLT PONS WESTCHESTER ASSOCIATION 250 PARK AVENUE NEWYORK
BUSHRANGER BETTER THAN ANY HORSE HERE BEST UNEXPOSED CHASER
IN AMERICA ABSOLUTELY SOUND FOUR YEAR OLD TWENTY THOUSAND
IMMEDIATE DELIVERY NO PRICE ONLY MY RETIREMENT FROM STEEPLE-
CHASING AZUCAR SOLD LAST WEEK
WIDENER

Telephone: HAnover 2-1811 To secure prompt action on inquiries, this original RADIOGRAM should be presented at the office of R.C.A. COMMUNICATIONS, Inc. In telephone inquiries quote the number preceding the place of origin.

Negotiations in five telegrams.

From Montpelier Stud in Gordonsville, Virginia, Mrs. Marion duPont Somerville is asking Widener about steeplechase prospects. Grandfather mediates between train trips to New York and Maryland.

#ONE
JUL 20 MONTPELIER STATION
TO BELAIR MD ADOLPHE PONS
KINDLY QUOTE LOWEST INDIVIDUAL FIGURE
ON BUSHRANGER FOR IMMEDIATE SALE =
FROM MARION SOMERVILLE

#TWO
JUL 23 CABLE NIGHT LETTER
TO WIDENER RITZHOTEL PARIS
PLEASE CABLE ME WESTCHESTER OFFICE
LOWEST PRICE BUSHRANGER
IMMEDIATE DELIVERY FOR MRS. SOMERVILLE
REGARDS ADOLPHE PONS

#THREE
JUL 25 RADIOGRAM
TO WESTCHESTER ASSOCIATION NEW YORK
BUSHRANGER ABSOLUTELY SOUND FOUR-YEAR-OLD
TWENTY THOUSAND
AZUCAR SOLD LAST WEEK

#FOUR
JUL 25 DAY LETTER
TO MRS. T. H. SOMERVILLE
MR. WIDENER REPLIES TWENTY THOUSAND
PLEASE ADVISE

#FIVE
JUL 25
TO A. PONS
ALL STEEPLE CHASE STAKES GREATLY REDUCED
WOULD NOT WARRANT PAYING
SUCH A PRICE FOR BUSHRANGER =
MARION SOMERVILLE

Widener does not sell Bushranger; instead, he wins the 1936 American Grand National with him. Bushranger fractures a leg schooling at Belmont in 1937 and is put down. Thirty years later, he enters the National Museum of Racing Hall of Fame. In reverse engineering, the steeplechaser Azucar jumps back into flat racing, where in 1935, he wins the inaugural Santa Anita Handicap—at one hundred thousand dollars, the richest race in the world.

Marion duPont Somerville divorces Thomas Hugh Somerville and marries Randolph Scott, taciturn star of Western movies and—in true Hollywood twist—Somerville's best man in the former marriage. Mrs. Scott wins the English Grand National in 1939 with Man o' War's son Battleship, who jumps into the Hall of Fame in 1969.

Five telegrams from one hundred years ago. In call-and-response style. In just under one hundred words. Bound by paperclips rusted red with time. The least words in their best order.

OBSERVATION ROOM

A vintage brass thermometer in the garret reads fifty degrees. Baseboard heat is no match for northeast winds whistling inside the double-hung windows, where lead-weight pulleys hold heavy frames of blown glass.

Moon full last night. Pregnant mares, heavy with water weight, feel gravitational pull. First wave of sixty in-foal mares settle in oversized stalls of the lower barn. Most imminent of the mares are bedded deep in yellow straw in Airflame's Barn, retrofitted into a modern equine maternity ward—rubber walls, padded floors pitched to drains. Hospital-grade improvements.

From this third-floor perch, the village of Country Life opens below: repurposed Quaker-built foaling barns, broodmare barns, tenant houses, farmhouses, lofts. Country Life, a company town. Building racehorses from the ground up since 1933, same as it ever was, same as it ever was.

Part 3

THE DEVIL YOU SAY

Just now I saw Dad. In the Spuyten Duyvil, that infamous Saratoga watering hole on the Fasig-Tipton Company's sales grounds. Dutch for "spitting devil." A name for a body of water downstate, around New York City. Dad was scribbling out a letter with pedigree notes about a four-year-old filly.

> Segment '48. By Some Chance. Out of Segula, by Johnstown out of Sekhmet. 2yo 1/2-sister Sabette, by Alsab.

A month later, here comes the reply:

> Dr. Robert B. Rakow
> Podiatrist
> 7512 Bay Parkway, Brooklyn 14, NY.
>
> September 16, 1952
>
> Dear Mr. Pons:
> In accordance with our talk at Saratoga this past August, I am shipping to you my mare Segment.

This is three years before Segment's half-brother Nashua becomes Horse of the Year, before his victory over Swaps in a celebrated match race.

"I picked up Nashua's sister in a bar," I can hear Dad say. I find a column written by sportswriter Snowden Carter of the Baltimore *Evening Sun*:

> October 12, 1954: When you catch two successful horse breeders in fatigue clothes mucking out stalls on a Saturday morning,

Adolphe Pons at the microphone.

> the sight is enough to make a man wonder "what kind of game is this?"
>
> Both John and Joe Pons knew why a reporter was visiting. They owned a half-sister to Nashua, in foal to Occupy. And it was Nashua who Saturday won the Belmont Futurity.

Newspaper articles are icebergs of cold news: three-quarters of the story lies beneath the surface. Research sparks them back to life. Like Dad's letter to Dr. Rakow. On evenings when I am thawing out decades-old news, I hate to see that evening sun go down, the sky turning pink to purple to black, so I experiment with that old Hemingway tactic—to quit where you can easily pick the story back up. Next morning, I icepick my way back into Segment's story.

Dad is making a longshot bet when he lays out a no-cash proposal to Dr. Rakow in 1952. Segment was a broken-down racemare: only three wins in forty-eight starts, only $9,625 in earnings. But Dad saw gold in the old William Woodward, Sr.'s broodmare band on the bottom line of the pedigree, while on the top line, August Belmont's influence: Segment's sire, Some Chance, was by Chance Play, by Fair Play, sire of the greatest horse in history, Man o' War. At no expense to Rakow—no board, no stud fee, no vet bills—the good doctor would receive the first foal from a 1953 mating to Lochinvar. Title to the mare, though, would belong to Country Life.

Comes the influence of Woodward's broodmare families. Segment's dam Segula is the mother of three-year-old filly Sabette, who wins the 1953 Alabama Stakes. Segula's two-year-old colt Nashua becomes 1954 juvenile champion. Anxiously, Dad awaits Segment's 1955 baby. Just when the family can't get any hotter, Segment's produce-record sputters: Dead foals in 1955 and 1956.

"I think that's when a client of Downey Bonsal buys the mare from us," says brother Mike. I scan Dad's diaries from those years, find breeding dates for Segment but no mention of a sale. Yet Mike must be right. In twelve-hour drives with Dad to Louisville for a score of Kentucky Derbies, Mike was wide awake at the wheel, enthralled by Dad's oral histories of the farm.

Much of this unlikely story of nags-to-riches feels bittersweet. Dad never would have sold a sister to Nashua had he been able to counter his older brother's majority rule. Why persevere with a mare who has delivered two dead foals in a row? I can hear Uncle Johnny, in that nasal know-it-all tone, as he tells Dad: "Now Joe, *it's time to sell.*" Of course, I dramatize everything because I loved Dad so much. I cry just reading the last line of Hemingway's "My Old Man," told by the son of a horseman:

"Seems like when they get started, they don't leave a guy nothing."

HONOR

To understand my dad, I first need to understand his dad, a French immigrant who became an assimilated New Yorker. In a documentary simply called *New York*, Brooklyn-born author Pete Hamill tells of his Irish immigrant father, a factory worker who had lost a leg:

> And I heard him weeping in the dark around 1 o'clock in the morning and I knew that no matter what I ever did . . . that I had to honor that pain. I think that's what the children of immigrants do, all of us. We honor their pain for the rest of our lives.

Grandfather holds this farm together through the Great Depression and then through World War II, but he is nearing his end, and he knows it. He needs his boys back. To honor his wish, Dad returns to the farm after the war. He musters out with the rank of private, not a colonel like brothers Addie and John. But his honorable discharge papers from four years in the Army are here in this room, and he was proud to have served. He had been stationed at Nebraska's Fort Robinson, a US Cavalry outpost inculcated with the lore of Indian Wars, the fort where Crazy Horse was bayoneted to death by soldiers guarding him.

Crazy Horse was revered by the Sioux for his prescient visions. Thoroughbred horsemen are revered for their vision if they can take unproven colts and make them into successful stallions. Prescience of a commercial kind. To Country Life in the 1960s, Dad recruits a colt named Big Brave, out of a mare named Sequoia. His vision proves out. Big Brave has fifteen precocious two-year-old winners in his very first crop. His pedigree earns national prominence in 1973 when his half-brother Sham stalks Secretariat through the Triple Crown.

Dad names a Big Brave colt "Fort Robinson." In a winner's circle photo from a distant day at Bowie Race Track, Fort Robinson carries the farm's orange and blue silks to victory.

The win photo is from March of 1978, colors fading. I send it out to be digitized, to be restored, a happy image of Dad for his grandchildren and

Big Brave.

Fort Robinson alum Joe Pons in the winner's circle with the homebred colt named for his World War II Nebraska outpost.

beyond—just some small way to honor him, yet it feels so personal. His war experience. The fort where he served. The legend of Crazy Horse, then the horse Big Brave. It's like that documentary film technique, when the camera zooms into a face in a photograph, then zooms out to expand the story being told by the narrator.

"Let me tell you kids the story of Fort Robinson."

RACEHORSE MEN

A son of our stallion Mosler named Hello Hot Rod may run in the one-hundred-thousand-dollar Jimmy Winkfield Stakes at Aqueduct, first New York prep in the run-up to the Kentucky Derby. Knowing nothing about Jimmy Winkfield, I grab down reference materials. Winkfield was a Black jockey who won the Derby in 1901 and 1902. Soon thereafter, Jim Crow laws drove Black riders and trainers from America. Winkfield steams across the Atlantic, concludes a brilliant career as the darling of French racing—known as *le blackman*, writes Katherine C. Mooney in her book *Race Horse Men: How Slavery and Freedom Were Made at the Racetrack*. I go from knowing nothing to being glibly conversant about Winkfield, homeschooled once again by this third-floor farmhouse library.

Back and forth in time I go. Two dozen photos of 1930s farm life tip out of a shoebox. In one, Uncle Johnny's gray house looms ghostly white across a field. In another, a foal passes in front of a long-gone wing of the Country Life farmhouse: Grandfather's studio, his office. No one now living had ever seen this missing wing, torn down to build a two-story newlyweds apartment when Mom and Dad marry in 1950. In a third, a gray mare grazes in the field nearest the house. I look out the windows to see a gray mare we just bought in Kentucky in the same field, in the same spot. For a trick second, she is the gray mare from the old photo, so strong is the pull of the past.

Out I go for some fresh air. I check in on the two mares due soonest, asleep in the deep yellow straw of Airflame's Barn, exhaling loudly, their breathing burdened by their enormous bellies.

Dad and Uncle Johnny night-watched in the days before foaling cameras. These days, a tack-room camera displays eight stalls on a Foal Cam. It's like "Hollywood Squares," with equine guests in the grids. Images of our pregnant mares stream out across the world, viewable on cell phones, lap-

In background appears the long-gone wing of Grandfather's office.

tops, iPads, television screens. Devoted fans of this late-night horse show, owners of mares—intermittent insomniacs all—watch the Wi-Fi feed from wherever. When a mare is foaling, Country Life General Manager Christy Holden isolates Camera One just on that stall, and reality TV takes over.

With begrudging admiration, my older brother Andrew often referred to Dad and Uncle Johnny as the "Old Boys." What would the Old Boys have thought of this digital age? They would have enjoyed watching our Foal Cam from warm kitchens. I shiver just imagining their nightly vigils, banging on barn pipes to signal to the house that a mare was foaling. How could I not feel the ancient cold when reading Uncle Johnny's diary?

February 4, 1936

Sleet and rain.
Very icy underfoot.
All horses in the barn.

BIGGER THINGS

Hundred-year-old ash trees outside garret windows are chain-sawed to the ground. Taller than this farmhouse—all of them, now gone, owing to a tiny beetle. I run my fingers across twisted trails in the bark where the emerald ash borer bored. Something so little to bring down something so big. By month's end, the loss of a few trees seemed no longer to matter. For three years, I've worked in a room of letter-writers who endured a great depression sandwiched between two world wars. I've admired their immense courage but only in the abstract. Now it's my turn to write letters during a world at war—against a virus. For someone to look back on. Maybe from this room, perhaps once again shaded by towering ash trees, hopefully resistant to disease.

A caravan of sand-colored National Guard vehicles shares the slow lanes of Interstate 95 with me. I am driving the horse van to Laurel to pick up a pair of race fillies shipping home for some unexpected turnout time. Laurel canceled racing yesterday—indefinitely. The security guard at the Stable Gate calls up to me in the cab of the horse van.

"Have you traveled out of the country in the last twenty-one days?"

No.

"Have you been in contact with anyone who has traveled out of the country in the last twenty-one days?"

No.

"Have you had any symptoms of the flu? Coughing?"

No.

"Have you got a current Maryland racing license?"

Yes.

He examines my license, slaps an orange Maryland Jockey Club sticker on it, hands it back up.

"You're good for one week," he says, and waves me through.

Two grooms lead Bella Aurora and Virginia Beach up into the van. Like many horse people these days—breeding-shed crews steadying stallions atop mares, trainers giving jockeys a leg up, technicians holding horses for veterinarians, hotwalkers circling narrow shedrows—we are clearly violating the six-foot social distancing guideline. In tight quarters on the van, the grooms don't mention it. They back out after I set a spring-loaded steel bar horizontally across the chests of the two fillies. At that moment, a winch-truck drops a dumpster nearby. Startled, Bella Aurora hurtles backwards against the cab, Virginia Beach smacks hard against the bar. Tie chains hold. The bar blocks any escape. I hoist a hay net between the fillies, rub their foreheads as they grab anxiously at the alfalfa. We all settle. At the gate, I pass down a stable release form to the sentry guard, executed in triplicate. I see no National Guard trucks on my ride back to the farm, but that does not give me a sense of relief.

I WANT TO KNOW WHY

The third-floor balcony is stacked wedding-cake-like atop the second-floor porch atop the first-floor porch. This balcony has no door. You reach it on your hands and knees, dipping your head, dropping your back, a yoga move through double-hung windows. But if you want to make certain the automatic gate at the driveway is closed, you dive out headfirst, then stand up to look for trouble.

The farm's main driveway leads to Old Joppa Road—no longer a sleepy, cedar-lined shortcut but an express lane of interlopers off Interstate 95. One such driver recently pulled in the lane, shot a .22-caliber bullet into the glass sensor of the automatic gate, and drove off in the getaway car. Tell me please: Why would someone come onto a farm and shoot a gun at a gate?

Suddenly gun-shy, I fret about security. I climb headfirst onto the balcony. From this vantage, I stand where a photographer one hundred years ago took a memorable farm photo of a lone horse grazing winter grass. Spacious fields. Soaring sycamores. Matching pair of blue spruce. No hint of the outside world. In the Great Depression, strangers with bindles slung over their shoulders would walk up this driveway. My grandmother Mary MacNamara Pons, our "Nana," would wave them into the house, where she would throw another potato into the pot, as her Irish ancestors would say. The strangers would ask to work for their meal.

These are not those days. The outside world is closing in, and strangers carry guns.

THE USE OF FORCE

An unmarked black binder. Leather edges curled stiff. Despite my gentle efforts, the brittle binder cracks loudly, painfully, after being shut for one hundred years. I am reminded of the short story "The Use of Force," by William Carlos Williams when during a diphtheria epidemic, a doctor attempts to examine a young girl's throat. She refuses to open her mouth. A struggle ensues. I feel similar resistance opening this black binder. It flattens out stiff as an opened oyster. Inside, paper pearls: names of the foals, stallions, and mares of Grandfather's clients from the 1920s.

First name up, Averell Harriman's mare Flaminia, the mother of Flamante, who Grandfather will breed to Ariel in 1933, the mating that produces Airflame, the fastest horse in the world in 1936—if all races were only three furlongs. Flaminia appears in volume XV of August Belmont's American Stud Books. I marvel at the minutiae meticulously noted by long-dead clerks of The Jockey Club:

*Flaminia, b., 1919; imported (in 1926) by Jos. E. Widener; owned by Lenox Stud, New York, N. Y. By Sunstar. (English Stud Book, vol. 26, page 320.)
1st dam Tiberia, by Bend Or.
1926 b. f. *FLAMANTE, by Flamboyant

Ghostwriters sidle along the attic wall, declare to the air: "We never apologize for being precise." In alphabetical tabs, Grandfather's binder lists the players in the Golden Age of Racing.

B: Brookmeade Stable, Isabel Dodge Sloane.

C: Cosden, Alfred H., owner of 1928 Belmont Stakes winner Vito.

. . .

. . .

. . .

G: Glen Riddle Farms, the Report of Foals of 1928.

How's this for a few nights in the foaling barn of Riddle's Faraway Farms?

April 6, chestnut filly by Man o' War
April 11, chestnut colt by Man o' War
April 12, chestnut colt by Man o' War
April 15, chestnut colt by Man o' War
April 24, bay filly by Man o' War

Imagine being farm manager Elizabeth Daingerfield, those next-morning telegrams to Riddle in Philadelphia. "Another beautiful foal by Man o' War!" I find some saddle soap, lather up the leather of the old black binder, pull down another brittle old book.

ATTACKS

Vintage medical bible: *Veterinary Notes For Horse Owners*. Grandfather owned a copy of the ninth edition, printed in London in 1921, written by M. Horace Hayes, late captain of the British regiment "The Buffs." I picture Captain Hayes on horseback in the Boer Wars of the late 1800s. In *Veterinary Notes*, he raises his sword against diseases of his time, such archaic names: Glanders, Farcy, Moon Blindness, Catarrh, Staggers, Immobilité. Grandfather's high esteem for *Veterinary Notes*? If lost in the midnight haste of equine emergencies, he wants it back. He swirls "Property of Adolphe Pons" inside the cover.

Grandfather's copy is ragged, its spine broken. Horseshoe-shaped bleach-stains mar its cover. It needs rebinding. On this one-hundredth anniversary of Captain Hayes' ninth edition, I send it off to the book seamstress in Baltimore. Time for a new uniform for this old soldier. I tip my cap to the captain on his understanding of viruses.

"The attack will have run part of its course before its existence is suspected."

KITTY'S BACK

Pandemic isolation is eased by panorama of farm life. Seen through blown-glass windows, mares and foals ripple as they run. From the attic height, I can almost see the corners of the farm: the boulder midstream in Winters Run, the concrete marker deep in the woods below the stallion paddocks. I am surrounded by home. All so quiet. Hardly a car on Route 1, on Old Joppa, on meandering farm lanes. Only vital vehicles. A veterinarian's pickup. A flatbed trailer of bright yellow straw.

When the governor of Maryland issued a mandatory stay-at-home order on March 30, many mares were already here for breeding, for foaling. Most of us who work on the farm live here. The directive from the state insists that we work from home. I feel so lucky to comply, so fortunate for quiet time to study this treasure of never-before-seen, primary source material.

Every Saturday morning for a year prior to beginning this book, I would heft three stiff dry-rotted cardboard boxes up the forty-two stairs from basement to attic. Just three boxes, so not to overwhelm my time-consuming task of sifting and sorting. I was rewarded by every unearthed discovery, to wit:

In the spring of 1964, Mrs. William Haggin ("Kitty") Perry sends a thank-you note to Dad after his letter of condolence over the loss of champion filly Lamb Chop. I look for context, consult *The American Racing Manual*, find the account of the 1964 Charles H. Strub Stakes at Santa Anita. Iconic columnist Charles Hatton tells the tragic tale:

> Gun Bow opened up . . . while Lamb Chop broke down amid cries of empathy. The 1963 three-year-old filly champion who was bred by A. B. Hancock and raced for W. Haggin Perry shattered an ankle and was humanely destroyed.

The Hancock-Perry partnership had just sent Big Brave to stand here.

"We do hope that Big Brave is behaving like a Big Boy," Kitty writes. "Maybe we can stop by someday when he isn't busy holding court."

Big Brave's co-owner William Haggin Perry was the great-grandson of James Ben Ali Haggin, a contemporary of both August Belmont I and II. Grandfather's books include two copies of Haggin's gold-lettered 1905 *Thoroughbreds of Rancho del Paso*—listing 545 broodmares and thirty stallions who roamed Haggin's forty-thousand-acre California ranch at the turn of the century. Haggin also owned Elmendorf Farm in Kentucky, expanding the historic stud to ten thousand acres.

Grandfather's client Joseph E. Widener buys Elmendorf in the 1920s. On land later to become Normandy Farm, Widener buries Man o' War's sire and dam: Fair Play next to Mahubah. In the 1950s, Elmendorf passes to New York City dress manufacturer Maxwell H. Gluck, founder of the University of Kentucky's Gluck Equine Research Center. In the mid-1960s, Gluck's Elmendorf homebred Rash Prince joins Big Brave in the stallion barn here. Their stud fees put a generation of farm boys through college. All these threads tease out of Kitty Perry's brief note, her exquisite handwriting on stationery in the yellow and blue of the Perry silks:

> The sympathy extended to us by our friends and Lamb Chop's admirers has been a tremendous comfort and we are grateful beyond words. Our most sincere thanks, Joe.
>
> As ever,
Kitty
April 25, 1964

Rash Prince on the lunge line at Country Life Farm, as seen on the February 1970 cover of The Maryland Horse.

LA MÊME CHOSE

Title page of the 1886 reference book *Horse-Racing in France* is stained by the acids from a newsprint column describing an incident just before World War I.

```
  FRENCH HORSES ARE DISQUALIFIED WHEN "DOPING" IS
PROVED
  PRIZE MONEY WON IS DECLARED FORFEITED
```

Today's racing papers:

```
$20-MILLION SAUDI CUP PURSE WITHHELD
INVESTIGATION INTO RICHEST RACE IN THE WORLD
```

Next book up: the 1911 French Stallion Register—*Étalons de France*. To France have flocked prominent American breeders and owners of that day after an anti-gambling virus shuttered New York tracks. August Belmont sends his Kentucky stallion Ethelbert, winner of the Metropolitan Handicap in 1900, to stand stud at his Haras de Villers in France. Grandfather travels overseas to oversee Ethelbert.

Named for the brother of King Alfred the Great of ninth-century England, Ethelbert sires a queen of Thoroughbred breeding: the great broodmare Quelle Chance. Her name means "How Lucky." She will be the most expensive mare in the Belmont dispersal even though she never leaves France, where she is fulfilling an assignation with international star Epinard.

E. E. Coussell of the British Bloodstock Agency, on Widener's behalf, bids forty-five thousand dollars for Quelle Chance. Widener had bought her from the Belmont estate six months earlier. He simply had her appraised by the market the day of the Belmont dispersal, and Coussell's bid represented a buyback. Sharp business to hang onto her. Quelle Chance's two-year-old of that year is Chance Play, who will become a two-time leading American sire following his Horse of the Year racing career for Log Cabin Stable. Quelle Chance's yearling, Chance Shot, also from the Belmont estate sale, will win the 1927 Belmont Stakes in Widener's silks.

The stodgy sounding name of Quelle Chance's sire Ethelbert triggered this dive into horse history. I find a 1919 letter from Grandfather to Hall of Fame trainer George Odom. They've gone in halves to race a colt named Beaumaris, a half-brother to Quelle Chance.

July 30th

Dear Odom:
I suppose we will have to be very careful with the horse, as I understand he is very well touted. We better not put him in selling races or we might lose him.

Down the centuries, the fear of every owner is to lose a nice horse in a claiming race—known in Grandfather's era as a "selling race." When you risk a horse in a claiming race, a card laid is a card played. *Le même chose.* The rules have not changed.

HOPE THROUGH HISTORY

As Country Life endures the pandemic, primary source materials provide examples of similar challenges. Of the Spanish flu at the end of World War I, Grandfather writes to his sister in France, sharing news of their brother Etienne.

November 2, 1918

My dear Marie,
There were thousands of deaths every day. Etienne was sick for three weeks.

During the Great Depression, Grandfather sends this imploring update to Belmont's widow:

August 15, 1933

Dear Mrs. Belmont,
A number of small breeders will go broke. Large stud fees are a thing of the past. Mrs. Belmont, would you recommend my brother Etienne to some position? He has been out of work since February. He lost all his money in the stock market. He is a nervous wreck going place to place and always receiving the same answer.

During a polio epidemic when Dad was a boy, his legs were partially paralyzed. He will walk with a listing gait the rest of his life. I find this card in his wallet—among his effects, as they say. It was issued by the Maryland Medical Society:

October 1, 1962

This is your record of vaccination against TYPE 1 POLIOMYELITIS. Type II will be given in November, and Type III in January 1963. You need all three types to give full protection.

During the Cuban Missile Crisis, Dad receives this directive from the Civil Defense Agency:

1964

Effective on attack, this form shall be employed by LOCAL DIRECTORS for emergency requisition in the name of the state of Maryland.

Confident the farm will continue to operate even after nuclear war, Dad lists necessities: fuel for tractors, food for children, bedrolls to sleep on in root cellars. He was incapable of being fatalistic for very long, and I imagine him saying "Oh, to hell with it" before driving off to the American Legion to play poker with his World War II buddies. Ironic that a pair of howitzers from World War I—the war to end all wars but didn't—stands sentry at the Legion entrance, lo these many wars later.

VOICES CARRY

Downed trees from an overnight storm knock out electricity. No lights on kitchen stoves to make coffee. No fans whirring in windows. No distraction from television news. In the stillness, I hear streams and birds and frogs. I walk to work with the sun rising. This is the Thursday before what would have been Preakness Saturday. Every May since 1961, when Saggy's son Carry Back won the Kentucky Derby, we've hosted a Preakness Party two evenings before Baltimore's famous race. The 145th running of the Preakness is now postponed to October 3.

Mom originally called it "The Press Party." Sportswriters in town for Carry Back's classic filled her guest list. She would handwrite every invitation in blue ink, her perfect penmanship unwavering through a hundred repetitions. Guests felt her personal touch, replied by return mail. For weeks after "The Press Party," thoughtful thank-you notes filled Mom's mailbox from well-fed and certainly well-watered members of racing's Fourth Estate.

(Left-to-right) The evening of the 1964 Preakness Party: sister Alice (age 5); Carry Back's owners Katherine and Jack Price; Country Life's 15-year-old broodmare The Heater, held by sister Norah (age 12); black colt by Carry Back later named Back Burner, held by the author (age 9); press members Gene Ward and Joe Nichols (back wall).

In 1979, the year of Spectacular Bid's Preakness, the winners of Pimlico's venerable Old Hilltop Award assembled for a photo at the Alibi Breakfast the day before the classic:

Win Elliot, the voice of horse racing on WCBS Radio in New York
Joseph Hirsch, *Daily Racing Form*
Joseph B. Kelly, *Washington Star*
Charles Lamb, *Baltimore News American*
Robert Maisel, *Baltimore Sun*
Barney Nagler, *Daily Racing Form*
William G. Phillips, *Daily Racing Form*
Red Smith, *New York Times*
Whitney Tower, *Classic Magazine, Sports Illustrated*

I stare at their faces like I'm in a wax museum of Turf Writers. I'm a kid again. Party music drifts up the stairwells from Mom's upright player

White fences, white gravel driveway at Country Life in the 1960s.

piano, pumping out a drunken singalong of "Peg o' My Heart." Ice boys like me dash down basement steps to a freezer chest, to resupply bartenders as racing stories flow. What else for my imagination to do on this party-less night but find fascination in history? I look out through balcony balustrades to the front yard. It is full of people I cannot see. I hear them, though, speaking through a cassette player on the wraparound porch, a recording of the 1965 Preakness Party broadcast by WVOB Radio, acronym for the "Voice of Bel Air."

Pulitzer Prize–winner Red Smith: "I started at the Preakness long before I ever got to the Derby."

Sports Illustrated's Whitney Tower: "This is one of the fastest growing Thoroughbred communities in America."

Mellifluous Win Elliot: "How beautiful this countryside is. They talk about the Bluegrass, but I enjoy the green, and may it forever remain as verdant as it is tonight."

Jack Whitaker of CBS: "These fences are just so white, and there is a full moon tonight, and anybody not having a good time, it's their own fault."

In the ether, I hear Mom greeting them all personally, individually.

"Welcome to *The* Preakness Party."

Part 4

THE LANGUAGE OF GHOSTS

On my walk to work this morning, I startled a pair of deer in the woods by a spring. They soared over four-board fences, hard hooves thwacking the locust posts like gunfire. Minutes later, I flicked on the lights in the attic. Sleeping spirits startled but didn't leap away. I sense that they regard me as a sort of custodian. I freshen the workplace, run a vacuum to scoop up bits of brittle letters.

"What can I do for you today?" I call out to the residents as a baseboard heater ticks to life. They show me faces from the 1940s reversed out of negatives. White-washed fences appear tarred black. A white yearling being ridden by a white rider is in life a black yearling ridden by a Black rider: Gene Fisher, Grandfather's top stallion groom, top exercise rider, toppled by drink in the 1960s.

A monotone mare pauses at a black salt block. Of course, the salt block is white. A gentleman in a white suit holds a dog treat waist high for a bouncing beagle. That's Grandfather in his trademark three-piece. Dad's glasses shine white. They weren't. When I show the negatives to my family, they make out shapes of familiar faces, guess names out loud, like this is a game show.

No 1940s negative of the front field Uncle Johnny sold in the 1970s, so no painful pang of loss. If that beautiful bottom field were photographed today? A two-story, mixed-use office development, on whose long horizontal roofline I have always wanted to paint the words Old Grand-Dad—for the bourbon I blame for the loss of that lovely land.

Gene Fisher on a yearling in the 1940s.

SIGNS OF THE TIME

In the mid-1970s, manila envelopes bearing the return address of the financial firm Bert Walker founded are poured out onto the breakfast room table. You know it is a serious day on the farm when Dad carries around G. H. Walker & Co. stationery. But as Ben Franklin said: "Pour your purse into your mind and no one can ever take it from you." Dad pours his purse into our minds; he sold those stocks to pay for our education.

On a wainscoted wall in the garret, I push-pin tuition bills marked PAID from the University of Virginia, from The John Carroll High School, to remind me of what Dad sacrificed when he put his purse into my mind. Not easy times, the 1970s. Neither Dad nor Uncle Johnny had enlisted in AA yet. Uncle Johnny, majority owner of the stock of Country Life Farm, Inc., looked at the field at Route 1 and Old Joppa Road and saw dollar signs. This was the front field in which Grandfather put up the farm's first sign, arcing the name COUNTRY LIFE FARM above the straight-line smaller letters of THOROUGHBRED NURSERY, echoing his days as secretary of Nursery Stud. On a weekend home between college and law school, I am told by Uncle Johnny:

"Take down the sign tomorrow. The bulldozers are coming on Monday."

High school friend Kevin Kellar drives the ancient Farmall tractor. We dig out locust posts set in the ground in 1933. We pry the venerable sign off the posts and ride with it in a wooden manure wagon, like it's a family corpse journeying home in some dark Faulkner novel.

WARHORSES

This attic is like some know-it-all person, the type who tops everyone else's stories. Some days, it backs me into a corner, questions my competence to write. To overcome creative block, I fight a war with the room. No armistice this morning. I came up forty-two steps to write the story of a Preakness-less May in Maryland, how it felt to walk out onto an empty yard, hydrangea blooming in white snowballs, pink dogwood trees budding down a car-less driveway on the evening of the party-that-wasn't, just two days before the race-that-isn't. How bright and clean the old farm looked in the crystal spring air. The white house, the gray-blue decks of the stone porches, the green fields. How poignant the echoes of the past sounded in this beautiful yard. But the moment I set my fingers on this keyboard, up pops the peerless prose of John Hervey, effortlessly dashing off a short story in 1940 about the Battle of Dunkirk. Courtesy of *The Thoroughbred Record*:

> During the hurried horror of the evacuation from the Netherlands . . . the entire terrain at the mercy of the Nazis, under a rain of projectiles, like a scene from the Inferno, a man leading a magnificent chestnut stallion.
>
> The horse was lame and walked with difficulty. An officer said: "You'd better shoot that lame horse. You can never get him away."
>
> "Shoot him?" was the response from the French soldier. "That's Epinard! I'd rather shoot myself."

Greatest horse in France in 1923. Sportingly sent to America by Pierre Wertheimer in 1924 for a series of three international contests dreamed up by August Belmont. To be run at three different tracks: Belmont Park, Aqueduct, and Latonia. At Aqueduct, Epinard loses to Belmont's Ladkin by a nose.

I study a conformation photo of high-headed Ladkin and find the receipt from photographer Leonard S. Sutcliffe, for ten dollars. Then this letter from the Office of the Quartermaster General, June 25, 1941, a year after Dunkirk, six months before Pearl Harbor:

1937 Maryland Horse *Ladkin cover.*

Lt. John Pons
Reno Q. M. Depot
Fort Reno, Okla.

Dear Sir:

I take pleasure in expressing the appreciation of the War Department for your generous donation of the stallion LADKIN. This horse will be of great value to the breeding work being conducted by the Remount Division.

Edwin N. Hardy
Colonel, Q. M. C.

Hervey's elegy for Epinard foreshadows the fires about to engulf the entirety of Europe, the war that soon will take Grandfather's three sons away for years.

The living horse disappears in the hell of blood and fire which Nazism has made of the Old World. Let us not forget him in this one, where peace still reigns.

FROM FRONT YARD TO FIFTH AVENUE

Races that were canceled by COVID-19 at Colonial Downs in August are run at Laurel in October. Our aptly named Virginia Beach wins a rich race restricted to Virginia-breds: the M. Tyson Gilpin Stakes, named for a charismatic Fasig-Tipton chairman, a respected bloodstock agent. Virginia Beach, her flaxen tail flying, our orange and blue silks on the emerald grass course. The filly was bred by Mr. and Mrs. C. Oliver Iselin III—an oh-so-memorable name in attic archives. I rushed home to read their history. A New York banking family of the Gilded Age who summered in Newport, raced yachts against the Belmonts, won the *America*'s Cup three times. Freshly gleaned knowledge. This is how eminent racing historian Edward L. Bowen advised me to study the past:

"The best you can do is learn more and more about more and more until you know something about something."

I slide a lawn chair out the window and onto the third-floor balcony. I dive into David Black's *The King of Fifth Avenue: The Fortunes of August Belmont*, a biography of the first August Belmont. The book begins the evening of his arrival in New York City, at the height of the Panic of 1837, the city paralyzed. He is a twenty-three-year-old emissary of Europe's Rothschild banking family. It is Belmont's first night in America:

> From the harbor the night wind carried the hollow snap of canvas buckling in the breeze. People abroad in the streets seemed subdued, like citizens of a city suffering from plague.
>
> After the first shocks of fear, greed, and panic, people adapted to the disaster.

Over Country Life at any hour these days or nights, a helicopter will rip the air, ferrying victims of the virus to city hospitals, the *chop-chop-chop-chop-chop* of the rotors gearing down the valleys toward Baltimore. I play with John Donne's bell-tolling requiem, written as he battled spotted fever: Ask not for whom the helicopter lands. It lands for thee.

Free association thoughts are triggered by sounds. I am ten years old when a helicopter does, in fact, land in the front field, just below the sightline of the balcony on which I am reading the Belmont biography. Barnstorming pilot Col. Cloyce J. Tippett and his famous wife, Liz Whitney Tippett, have arrived. Tippett is the last of four husbands for Liz—a/k/a Mary Elizabeth Altemus, a/k/a Liz Whitney, demanding divorcee of sportsman John Hay "Jock" Whitney.

Liz Tippett visits Country Life Farm by helicopter, 1963.

It is an October six decades ago, 1963. Col. Tippett and Liz lifted off in their purple chopper from her two thousand-acre Llangollen Farm near Upperville, Virginia, and an hour later, rotors whirl to a stop here at Country Life. Local newspapers photograph the landing. Liz is here to see her stallion Correspondent, a son of Khaled, sire of 1956 Horse of the Year Swaps. Every stud farm wants a Khaled son. Correspondent was our second one. He filled the empty stall of the first: another Llangollen-owned stallion named Divine Comedy, who had died of a heart attack in April of 1963.

A complete dossier on glamourous Liz is found in attic files. Here she is, beautiful in a 1931 Franklin Voss portrait, riding her gray hunter bareback—no bridle, just a halter, just a shank, the casual pose she insisted upon. Here she is again, in a studio portrait, in an evening dress, looking over her shoulder, posing fetchingly, bare back. And there she is with Uncle Johnny at a horse show at the Front Royal Remount Depot. I find a letter from Grandfather to Liz in 1945, when racing was suspended, just as it is now:

My dear Mrs. Whitney:

This ban on racing is a terrible thing, especially for the "little fellows," and the only thing left for us is to breed in order to have nice yearlings when racing is back.

I hope you will consider the stallions I have standing.

Adolphe

Twenty years later, Liz is prodding Dad about lagging bookings to Correspondent:

Joe:

Why don't you work on Correspondent the way you did Mr. Hancock's horse Big Brave, as you told me his book is full?

Liz

Oblivious to the plummeting appeal of her aging broodmare band, she intensifies her demands in a 1965 letter listing forty-seven mares she insists Dad sell for her. Here's the produce of Mare 47, Witch Song, her name a portent of trouble brewing:

Slipped foal
Foal died
Barren
Merry Tune, by *Endeavour II, placed at 4
Foal put down
Barren
Barren
Barren

Who would buy such a star-crossed broodmare? This attic preserves records of galling examples of some clients' unreasonable expectations, but I learn pedigree lessons simply by researching Liz's mares. Witch Song's sire is named Stepenfetchit, which is what Liz is asking Dad to do. Stepenfetchit is by The Porter, by Polymelus, a hero in Homer's *Iliad*. Polymelus is trained by English legend John Porter, who also trained 1883 Epsom Derby winner St. Blaise, foundation stallion of the original Nursery Stud on Long Island. Porter trained 1899 English Triple Crown winner Flying Fox, whose slashing white face looks down at me from the living room wall in a photo by Newmarket's equine portraitist Clarence Hailey, camera wizard of his day.

This nightly education in the garret is not provided free of charge. The cost is hours of isolation in a room of spirits—or on a balcony outside that room—reading biographies, drilling into history books, hearing onion-skin letters snap in the breeze of a floor fan, imagining the challenges of those who came before.

SUCCESSION

Tonight, a break in the depressing pandemic newscasts bolsters spirits, like I'm listening to Radio Free Europe during World War II, news of a battle won. Sons and nephews and nieces, from Boston to Los Angeles to Denver to Baltimore, are all trading texts, attachments, Instagrams, about Governor Larry Hogan's administration passing Senate Bill 987, and the announcement of these headlines:

BILL TO RENOVATE PIMLICO, LAUREL PARK, PASSES INTO LAW

A huge sigh of relief for whoever runs Country Life after my generation joins the boxes of dead ancestors in the attic. When I walk among the mares in the fields, my step is lighter. Still, I startle foals sleeping in deep grass; they pop their heads up out of buttercups. Yearlings kick up their heels, rear up in play. The spring woods fill with fiddlehead ferns running down to Winters Run. Who could imagine Maryland without the beauty of her farms?

We make a product in these fields, in the staid old foaling barn, in the busy breeding shed. We make horses. Someday—we hope—they will be competing at the finest facilities in the country, though I'll believe it when I see it.

HERO WORSHIP

Peace in this pandemic. I float from letters to photos to books, pull down Brendan Boyd's *Racing Days* again. I write his descriptive words in notebook margins:

Raffish
Peripheral
Blind obeisance

After reading his essay "Truths," I handwrite his short sentences to absorb their style:

Winners leap out at him, like apparitions.
Athletics without competition is just exercise.
Money is, as Wallace Stevens told us, a kind of poetry.

```
   Losing a horse bludgeons all grooms—partially to a claim,
completely to death.
   The truth is far more chaotic.
```

Every sentence of Boyd's book should be required reading for participation in the horse business. At times, though, his trenchant essays overpower. I'm stunned reading about dead horses at county fairs or seeing grim photos of grimacing horses. I drop downstairs to the kitchen, catch the finish on television of a race from spectator-less Churchill Downs. A masked groom stands all alone with a horse in the Winner's Circle. It feels apocalyptic, a bad dream.

What would Boyd write today? Truths, of course. Here's one: Parking lots at Pimlico are filled with COVID-19 testing tents, Old Hilltop's zip code the hotspot in the city. Here's another: No family farm survives without help from every generation.

In the late 1940s, Uncle Johnny took the reins from his frail father and ran the farm until his interest waned in the 1960s. Dad stepped up, recruited stallions to stand here, represented the farm at sales in Kentucky, in Saratoga. It was a chaotic decade. Mom chronicled one day of it in a midnight letter.

Farm tour in 1967 with John Pons (center, straw hat) and visitors (teenage cousin Carol in white sweater on left).

Sunday 10-22-67

As if distractions at Country Life aren't wild enough, Laurel sponsored a Breeding Farm Tour today. . . . Great fun! For the last week, every sleepless night has been caused by nightmare scenes of pretty little girls in patent leather slippers and ruffled petticoats, envisioned with a few less than the right number of fingers. Lots of nice people don't know that some nice horses like to chew on things other than carrots and sugar. . . . Thus far, thank Heaven, no casualties here.

My nightmares for nothing. Six or seven hundred men, women, and children strolled the Farm today. Nary a gum wrapper or litter anywhere on the Farm.

Nobody smoked in the Barns, opened stall doors, climbed fences, went into the fields or even crossed the lawn. John Q. Public just generally behaved as he should have. Most unusual if what we hear or read of him is to be believed.

Remarkable, eh? Wouldn't it be nice if some talented scribe made mention of this phenomenon?

The clock ticks into the early 1970s. My sister Norah and my cousin Carol work side by side, like Civil War sisters on a farm where the brothers have marched off to enlist. Two women doing the work of four men, buying time for us boys to grow up, finish school.

Brother Andrew returns home at the worst of times, the late 1970s—Uncle Johnny a mean drunk by two o'clock in the afternoon, Dad a disaster by dinnertime. With love and heartbreak, Andrew endures the dysfunction of working for two alcoholics. Dad first, then Uncle Johnny, enter the AA program mere weeks apart in 1980. Prayers answered. A lesson for everyone: Don't ever give up on an alcoholic. These two sober brothers celebrate their one-year anniversary just as my brother Mike and I step to the plate in the 1980s, with younger sister Alice signing on as broodmare manager, excellent preparation for her eventual career as a Johns Hopkins nurse.

Compare and contrast. Dad in a Winner's Circle photo at Arlington Park in 1966. He's working on a stallion deal for a horse named Uncle Percy. His hair is trimmed, his sport coat is buttoned. He is happily "about my father's business," a biblical allusion he runs back often, always tongue-in-cheekily, always with a smile.

Sister Norah takes the reins with Joe Pons.

A photograph twelve years later, those difficult late 1970s. Norah and Dad are leading yearlings. She's twenty-six, looks sixteen. He's fifty-six, looks seventy-six, the booze exacting its price. Here's another truth: Every member of my family is a hero to me. A farm doesn't last decades in one family without heroes.

FAITH

What will the horse world of tomorrow look like? When the thought frightens me—that there will be no demand for the middle-market horses we raise out here in the boondocks of breeding, six hundred miles from the major league action of Kentucky, or that our racetracks will fail, or that we won't be able to defend ourselves against animal rights activists—I cast about for perspective, find it in a letter Mom wrote describing the arc of Dad's life.

> On May 23, 1980, Joe Pons entered an alcohol rehabilitation program. And that was the start of a new life for the entire family, but best of all for him.

On cue, I peer into a cardboard box of Dad's Day-Minder diaries. I flip open random entries. I know his secret code. "Brit JC." That means he has put off finishing The Jockey Club foal registrations for Delaware Park President Baird C. Brittingham. Not all the entries are in Dad's scrawling horse-bitten hand. I pause at the clarity of printed words by sister Alice.

Friday, January 2, 1981

Dad—

After I finish paying my bills, I'll send some $$ to you for the car—thanks—I love you—you made the holidays the most enjoyable ones I have ever had—I am truly proud of you—Keep the faith—Alice

Mom's letter, Dad's diaries, Alice's note: displays of character forged under years of pressure, endured one day at a time, heroic prose I am reading years after the fact.

YOU THERE

Walking down Man o' War Lane on the backstretch of Belmont Park. Over in the grandstand, the front office prepares for a renewal of the Belmont Stakes. Images from photos spring to mind. August Belmont II, dapper under a flat-topped straw hat. Grandfather on a paddock bench conversing with a racing official. Man o' War running clockwise in 1919, the opposite direction of today's racing. I drift over to a red-brick dormitory near the track kitchen, and I am fifteen years old again, transported back to the summer of 1970, when Dad dropped me off here, halfway to the end of Long Island. He had phoned up my godfather, a fine trainer named Jim Maloney, an old Remount pal who called Dad "Jofuss."

"Bring your boy up, Jofuss. I need another groom before we ship to Saratoga."

Fifty years later, I see myself fumbling with keys at the door to my room. I had never lived behind a lock. I remember every day of that summer. Every thought lines up like a poem in my head, the way Allen Ginsburg framed his classic "Howl."

You live in this dorm, no car, no way off the backstretch except on foot.

You think you can walk to New York City.

You never sleep well in that dirty, noisy hell.

Saratoga, 1970. The author at 16, Exorbitant at two.

You get out of bed at 4 a.m., doors banging all down the hall.

You dread having to use those bathrooms.

You are the rookie in Barn 9, and pay attention to Manny when he says: "These are your three horses. Before they come out of their stalls, remember, no straw in their tails, okay? Maloney hates straw in their tails."

You listen to Jose: "The barn hasn't won a race in three months. No good."

You feel the ghost of Jimmy Felts as Maloney's daughter Sheila tells you: "He was cutting through the tack room to the back shedrow, to pony a two-year-old out to the track. The pony slipped on the wooden floor. Jimmy's foot hung in a stirrup. He severed his spinal column. Didn't live twenty-four hours. *It was awful.*"

A horse named Dewan was the best in the barn. A five-year-old soon-to-be stallion. A blood-bay with a perfect flat forehead. I used to just stare at his face, the perfect symmetry of it. The most handsome horse I had ever seen. On a very hot Saturday in July, Dewan won the Brooklyn Handicap. Nobody thought any son of Bold Ruler could win at the testing distance of a mile and a quarter, except for his jockey Laffit Pincay. The next morning, Dewan stood motionless in his stall, his rump to the wall. He refused to move, even for his feed. Jose snapped Dewan to the tie-chain and handed me a jar of salve.

"Put this on his cuts."

I ducked under the webbing. My fingers were covered in sticky salve as I touched Dewan's flanks. He snapped to bite me, lifted his left hind leg to kick me. I felt the welts from Pincay's whip, the deep raw grooves in his beautiful bay skin. The salve stuck to my bloody hands. You think you know everything when you're fifteen years old. You don't know nothing.

CONTINUING ED

Nothing is more valuable in this attic than imagination. Rest my eyes anywhere. What do I see? An old black flag draped over the banister. Imprinted in white words: WELCOME PREAKNESS. Just another attic artifact. But have I ever examined this flag? Corners secured by brass grommets. Designed to fly from a pole at Pimlico. A white oval suggests a racetrack. Inside the oval, a rendition of an eighteenth-century race, those classic poses—three straight-backed Currier and Ives jockeys in long stirrups on rocking-chair horses whose legs stretch all the way forward, all the way back, not touching the track. It is the Pimlico logo, repeated in huge gold-painted horses flying high on the entrance side of the track's clubhouse.

I think of the photographs that proved that pose: Muybridge's 1878 collection "The Horse in Motion," his camera a zoopraxiscope—an unusual word I stumble over in articles about the Gilded Age, before Edison's motion pictures. The way the white ink dried on the jockeys, like they are riding in masks—so subliminal have covid precautions embedded in us.

Then I think of stories about jockeys. Hemingway's "My Old Man" sends me back to Dad's heart attack fifteen years ago, one floor below, as though Papa Hem was writing just for me:

> He looked so white and gone and so awfully dead. I loved my old man so much.

Then the brilliant gem "My Jockey" by Lucia Berlin, told from a nurse's point of view:

> I like working in Emergency—you meet real men, heroes. Firemen and jockeys . . . I get the jockeys because I speak Spanish.
>
> Munoz lay there, unconscious, a miniature Aztec god. He snorted softly. I stroked his fine back. It shuddered and shimmered like that of a splendid young colt.

What connects one letter, or one book, or one short story, to artifacts up here? How does it all thread together? No one can spend three years in a library without asking how the magic works.

ARTWORK

Drive out of Country Life after watching weanlings playing. Rattled by resumption of traffic on I-95. Arrive at Laurel at a checkpoint. A window slides open, and I push my owner's license through the gap. A guard I can't see stands in the dark, aims a thermometer pistol at my forehead, shoots me, checks the reading, then waves me in.

Magnificent horses ridden by tiny men in brightly colored silks stream past on the grass course, like some French impressionist dreamscape. All afternoon, not a single runner by our farm's stallions runs well. Who cares? I'm just happy to see the action. I'm just happy to be alive—unlike those ancestors I left behind in the attic this morning.

Back home by dusk. Come see. A bald eagle has fallen into a back field. Broken winged? Broken legged? The farm crew gathers round him to keep away the farm dogs. The Department of Natural Resources is alerted but never shows. Old Baldy starts crow-hopping downhill, gains momentum, lifts off to land in a low poplar branch.

Night falls.

By morning, Baldy's gone on the wind, everyone relieved by his recovery. Symbolic of a mending country. A sign of hope. Next day, I am driving the horse van across the Conowingo Dam. The Susquehanna River spills through flood gates. Spray flies skyward to windshield-wash the van. Bald eagles bank into updrafts, the river below running with shad. I look downstream toward Havre de Grace. A mile below the dam, equine artist Vaughn Flannery owned a farm he called Cockade. Emblem of a red rooster on Flannery's letters to Grandfather, every letter like a seashell to hold to my ear, to hear the past.

My dear Adolphe—
Sorry to be so long in signing this. All the best,

Vaughn Flannery

He is writing from his art studio on his farm, where he designed the USA emblem athletes wore in the 1932 Olympics. As I learn who Flannery was, I learn that "Art" was an Olympic event that year. Flannery earned fame for painting unscripted moments—horses loading onto a van, horses rubbed down after a workout. Last week, I found a moldy old print buried beneath other moldy old prints: "Daybreak, Old Pimlico," by Vaughn Flannery. I showed the print to the Coyle Studios restoration folks, who told me that the original framing was done by the Bendann Brothers, old Civil War photographers, the Matthew Bradys of Baltimore. Evidence that Grandfather valued this print. A rose-colored Pimlico, the yellow clubhouse past the finish line.

Plans for a new Pimlico pay no mind to the past. On my desk, I prop Flannery's freshly reframed print of old Pimlico at daybreak, hoping for a rose-colored future for the once-lovely racetrack—as unlikely as that seems.

ROOM OF ALWAYS

Taking a page from the fourteenth-century Italian poet Petrarch. While isolated in a cathedral during the Plague, Petrarch found letters written some thousand years earlier by the Roman philosopher Cicero. To counter his loneliness, Petrarch decided to write back to Cicero, to tell him about life during the Black Death.

Isolated in the attic in pandemic mode, I write back to Grandfather's letters. I tell him how yesterday's thunderstorm arrived in a wall of water. How I washed my hands in the rain. How I lifted my face into it and let it carry away all cares. How I was careful, though, to steer clear of the hillside where twenty-two-year-old riding horse Mosby's Raider caught a lightning bolt last month, the renderer's bill of $350 still smoking in my pocket.

I tell Grandfather how I researched the name "Petrarch" on The Jockey Club site, the name prefixed by a red P for Permanent. Petrarch: 1877 Ascot Gold Cup winner, an English stallion on the International List of Protected Names. I am certain he knew Petrarch from researching English bloodlines for August Belmont's equine acquisitions, but I certainly didn't know Petrarch, or why he deserved a prestigious Permanent name. And that is how this lofty library of letters—fifty feet above the farm—keeps luring me up these forty-two steps, to learn a little about a little so I know something about something.

SAGAMORE SPIRITS

Tracing pedigrees of horses, of people, it's a continuum. Eras intertwine. One moment my mind pictures yachts of the Iselins, of the Belmonts, slicing through roiling waters off Newport in the 1880s. The next moment, I am lifting free a thick file of 1930s letters between Grandfather and young Alfred Gwynne Vanderbilt, Jr. Grandfather's track record is spectacular in his dealings with Vanderbilt. In 1933, as Grandfather races future Hall of Famer Discovery under lease from Walter Salmon's Mereworth Stud, Vanderbilt makes inquiry. Salmon keeps raising his asking price.

"I brought my silks to Saratoga three times thinking I had the horse bought," Vanderbilt would say. Salmon reconsiders, sells Discovery for twenty-five thousand dollars late in the future champion's two-year-old season. Next horse up: Grandfather sells Airflame as a yearling to Vanderbilt. Airflame sets a world record in 1936 at Santa Anita as a two-year-old. Why then would Sagamore trainer Bud Stotler attempt to unload unwanted breeding stock on Grandfather?

My dear Mr. Stotler:

I have always been honest with you, and not gone after the almighty dollar just because it was AGV. Yet how is it that every time you deal with me you want to trade or exchange something? Again, you write to ask if I would trade Flamante—my top mare, the dam of Airflame—for two or three mares you would like to dispose of.

You know I am always willing to meet you halfway, but I must make both ends meet.

Hop in the way-back machine with me. In 1926, Col. Phil T. Chinn foaled out the filly That's That from the mating of High Time to Rush Box. To offset a debt to Grandfather, Chinn presented him with That's That, a full sister to the fabulously fast gelding Sarazen. Grandfather sold That's That to the Waggoner family's Three D's Stock Farm in Texas, who bred her to Chance Play to get Now What in 1937. When racing was banned in Texas in 1938, Grandfather bought back That's That and Now What and resold them to young Vanderbilt. Now What became champion two-year-old of 1939.

We are immersed in one-syllable two-word names. Now What bred to Bull Lea produced Next Move—champion in 1950 and 1952. Next Move to Native Dancer produced Good Move, the winner of the Spinaway Stakes in 1960. Sadly, a branch of this fantastic female line was snuffed out by two words: virus abortion. The disease was a plague upon the farm of Vanderbilt, as witnessed by Good Move's produce record:

1964 Foal born dead
1965 Broodmare aborted twins
1966 Broodmare aborted
1969 Broodmare aborted
1970 Heathen Ways, colt, by Idolater
1972 Broodmare aborted twins
1973 Broodmare aborted

Counting twins, that's eight dead babies from a Spinaway-winning daughter of a two-time champion mare. Imagine those next-morning phone calls from the farm manager, Vanderbilt testily picking up: "What now?"

Sagamore Farm's horse operation is shutting down. Miles of white board fencing have been crowbarred off posts which are then forklifted out of fields where once champions roamed. In place of horses, the farm has turned to growing ryegrass, an essential ingredient of a whiskey called Sagamore Spirit. What would Vanderbilt's spirit think?

The farm that Grandfather's horses did so much to launch in the 1930s is soon to be a headstone in horse history. The rolling Worthington Valley is almost devoid of Thoroughbreds, except for retired racehorses repurposed as foxhunters. Fancy modern castles to vanity now overlook unfenced fields manicured into immense lawns. Before Sagamore draws the shutters, I arrange a visit to its graveyard. Lichen grows on Discovery's headstone. I discern his 1931 birthdate, but not the year he died—1958, at twenty-seven years old. I imagine seeing him as a muscular two-year-old at Saratoga in 1933 carrying Grandfather's purple silks, gold braces on shoulders, purple cap, in the Hopeful Stakes. Discovery rests mere feet away from his grandson Native Dancer. Champion Bed o' Roses rests near her dam Good Thing. Now What lies near her daughter Next Move, descendants of Grandfather's mare That's That. I am humbled by so many headstones of horses I now know something about.

The spell of the graveyard stays with me. Power of suggestion at work. On my return to Country Life, on a path I've walked since childhood, I see things anew. A narrow stone I've never noticed rises chest high out of the creek bed, as though it is waiting to be engraved with the name of some handsomely antlered deer who, like me, simply went out for a walk. The straight-up stone is the same granite as Grandfather's in the cemetery of St. Ignatius Church six miles away.

I can only ever remember snips of poems. Shelley's "Ozymandias" pops into my mind from some distant English assignment, something about "trunkless legs of stone." I want to order Christmas wreaths for all the headstones in my head. That's the spirit, I concede to the season. Now that's the spirit.

LEAVING

The world connects in strands of prose. I read Anthony Doerr's short story "The Deep," about a boy growing up among Michigan salt miners during World War I:

> Every six months a miner is laid off, gets drafted, or dies, and is replaced by another, so that very early in his life Tom comes to see how the world continually drains itself of young men.

Names on the Wages pages of Grandfather's farm ledger during World War II bear witness to Doerr's words.

January 1942:

Odell Wyatt	$30
Jos. Davis	$12.50
Wayne Sells	$30

By October of the first full year for America in World War II, new names:

```
Wilmer Riley      $27.90
Clarence Hewitt   $25
John Brown        $25.10
```

Work. Worries. War. How the world continually drains itself of young men. Which makes me think of the young men from Mexico who keep this farm going. As per their seasonal visas, they must return to Mexico for two months each year. A farm party today to thank them. How unselfishly they've worked. That is my thought as Ellen arranges a group photo, as her camera clicks closed.

Our own young man—our older son Josh—flew home from his job out West for his thirtieth birthday. Bandana pulled high like a bank robber. His worry: to be Typhoid Mary to the old folks on the farm. His high school friends sing Happy Birthday. His mask prevents him blowing out candles, so he waves the head of a lacrosse stick at the cake. As he leaves for the airport, hood drawn like a monk, he is a young man on the move in today's America. It is heartbreaking to watch him drive out the lane—so we don't, because Mom was superstitious, and said never to watch leavings.

HERE IS NEW YORK

How does this room know my needs? Lost in lonely, lengthy reflection, I watch the laptop screen go blank, then return in a moment with photos of holidays a century ago, when Grandfather lived on Seventh Avenue in Brooklyn. Which prompts me to pull down a favorite book: *New York: An Anthology*, in which E. B. White in his essay "Here Is New York" writes that the city belongs to the "person who was born somewhere else and came in quest of something." He is describing my ancestors: the family of a French cook who toiled his life away in the hot kitchens of Belmont mansions. White writes: "No one should come to New York to live unless he is willing to be lucky." How lucky for Grandfather, though, to have been brought up in the Belmont household, where his ambition singled him out.

I learn a little about a little, such as, New York urban developer Robert Moses not only wanted to drive on a parkway, he wanted to park on a driveway—the one leading to Belmont's mansion on the Nursery Stud on Long Island. I find this letter to Grandfather written by Belmont's widow from her apartment at 1115 Fifth Avenue, in the Carnegie Hill section of Manhattan, on the Upper East Side—a lesson in city geography simply by studying return addresses.

> December 1st, 1939
>
> Dear Adolphe:
>
> Mr. Corner has just been to see me about title to a portion of the Nursery Farm property. I have not the slightest recollection of any claim being made to these eleven acres at the end of the main avenue. Your memory would be better than mine, and of course, goes further back.
>
> Sincerely yours,
> Eleanor Belmont

Mr. Corner asking about a corner? Sounds fishy to me. Was Mr. Corner a secret emissary acquiring rights-of-way for Mr. Moses? Those vestigial eleven acres of the original one thousand-acre Nursery Stud happened to lie in the path of the Southern State Parkway. I search the internet for Babylon, Long Island, find this:

> Historic Persons: August Belmont I. Noted 19th-century financier raised racing horses at his estate, which he founded in 1866. There is still a flat circular plot of ground just south of the Parkway where trainers worked horses. The former driveway of Belmont's estate was lined with tall pine trees still visible in the median of the Parkway.

From my desk in the attic, I am treetop-high to a line of pines screening Country Life from Old Joppa Road. My hands shudder, a foreboding that Harford County officials may someday impose a Moses-like right-of-way, perhaps in the name of eminent domain, to widen Old Joppa, to straighten Route 1, drivers flashing past, wondering where this lane of pines once led.

RIDING OUT

The first night, a fingernail moon falls fast, as though tied by a string to the sun. Next night, the moon lingers longer, grows larger. Third night, you think you see a man sitting in the crook of the crescent.

At noon, you stand on the hill above the river. Rapids shine like electric lights, splash like fountains in a plaza. Slender-trunked beech trees rise like steel-gray skyscrapers out of the watershed. Underfoot, the land rests. The horses of Country Life, except the old riding horses, are settled for the winter on our sister-farm, Merryland, eight miles south. Arthritic old racehorse Perfect Moon phlegmatically carries me down the lines of pines, until he hears a cellphone replay of a race bugling "Call to the Post." His ears prick. He forgets his broken knee, springs back to life.

By evening, I hear the steady drumbeat of my boots echoing up the forty-two stairs to the attic. I ask the ghosts to tell me about life in the horse business after Grandfather's death in 1951. Never one for work, Henry David Thoreau speaks up from a shelf near Walden Pond: "How many a poor immortal soul have I met well-nigh crushed and smothered . . . under one hundred acres of land." I take Thoreau with a grain of salt as I open another book: a mint-perfect edition of *American Race Horses of 1950.* Title page: By JOE H. PALMER. Copyright 1951 by THE SAGAMORE PRESS. The fifteenth volume of a series begun in 1936, generously underwritten by Vanderbilt. I stare at the book's vivid red-pink covers. Why, of course, it's cerise—the distinctive color of the three diamonds on Vanderbilt's famous racing silks. Inside, Palmer reports the racing news of 1950, the year Mom and Dad were married:

> Biggest change in the general structure of racing came in Maryland. Laurel Park was sold to Morris Schapiro of Baltimore. His son John D. Schapiro will serve as president, thus ending the close cooperation when Pimlico and Laurel were jointly owned, also forestalling the possibility of moving Pimlico's meeting.

Poor Pimlico. Forever a pawn. The Maryland Jockey Club—founded in 1743, the oldest racing association in America—these days is offering to give the land under Pimlico to Baltimore, but retain the rights to run the Preakness. All a part of the complex $375 million bond deal. While the Preakness may stay at Pimlico, the historic oval—the very dirt under the horses' feet—may be dramatically disturbed, shifted, rebuilt, to allow easy access to retail stores, or fire engines, or stretch limousines, who really knows why? Just twist the track like it's a lazy Susan, and *voila,* no one has to see the blighted neighborhoods on the south side. Why sacrifice 150 years of history? Every Preakness challenger competes with Man o' War, Citation, Secretariat—on the same track as those legends. Why would anyone want to move a track that hasn't moved since 1872? Who comes up with these ideas? In 1938, when Vanderbilt was president of the Maryland Jockey Club, he felt the spirit of his track's history:

> Pimlico is more than a dirt track bounded by four streets. It is an accepted American institution, devoted to the best interests of a great sport, graced by time, respected for its honorable past.

I shake my head. The difference between reading history and living history is that I know how the former ends.

"The meaning of life is that it stops," Kafka tells the garret gang, as if they hadn't figured that out. I run hot water into a sink, wash my hands free of the dust of musty old letters. The meaning of life sends me skipping down the forty-two stairs to burst out onto this beautiful old farm—just happy to exist in this moment.

SPIRITS OF CHRISTMAS PRESENT

Christmas Day can be bittersweet if I let it, so I work at being unsentimental. Fact: Grandfather has been gone exactly sixty-eight years. That's also how long he lived. That full-circle fact came to me in my sleep last night, as did this: That I'm as old as he was when he died. I awoke to a full moon, a feeling of symmetry.

Today in the attic, I found Grandfather's grade school homework from St. Ann's Academy. English grammar. Latin roots. Arithmetic. His handwriting is fluid, stunning, even at that age. Elementary lessons he never forgot prepared him for homework of a higher order; here's his precise reconciliation of the sixty-five broodmares who grossed $641,000 in the Nursery Stud dispersal in 1925.

Then I find his projections for the operation of this farm before buying it in 1933. In the uncertainty of the Great Depression, he writes to a fellow horseman:

> If I purchase this property, I intend to run it as a Thoroughbred breeding establishment on a commercial basis. If times improve, and we all feel they will, I am certain I can make a profit. If things get worse, none of us will care anyway.

On Christmas Days in the past, Dad would lead us out of church, five children strung out duckling-like behind him. He would walk across the grass to his parents' graves, where he would make a hasty sign of the cross. We would imitate his rote religious act and bless ourselves, too. Today, I retraced Dad's footsteps through the cemetery to find family headstones: chiseled in granite, the dates of births and deaths—a bit of fact-checking for me as I close out this record of the lives of ancestors.

"What have you learned?" Grandfather's spirit breaks the silence.

"Oh!" I reply, startled out of my reverie. "Well, for one, that history connects everything." It's so easy to telepath in a graveyard. "And maybe, secondly, that hard times come, and hard times go."

"Precisely," I feel him say.

Back at Country Life, I walk up the hillside where we spread Dad's ashes two decades ago. I make a sign of the cross, self-consciously, sort of the way family members mumble "*Love you*" hastily, yet no less sincerely. On return to the farm below, I stand in the front yard and look up three stories to the balcony outside the garret. I imagine Dad smiling down from the railing, that Hamlet-to-father moment, Ghost-Dad riding the ramparts.

"Get back to work, sonny boy."

Dad's laughter rides out on the winter wind. In a twist on his favorite line of irreverence, I look up and tell him: "I must be about my grandfather's business."

On my walk back home, I check on the horses in the lower barn. All quiet on the Christmas front. Then I'm out the back of the barn headed for the banks of Winters Run. I hear the rapids running through the woods, running down the ages. I feel as though a cloud full of ghosts is following me. "We've got more stories for your book," they volunteer.

"No," I reply. "Tell me after New Year's, okay? Can it wait?"

I turn around to feel them fly back to the attic, once again to conceal themselves behind those honey-colored closet doors. My imagination runneth over. After three years of studying in their presence, I feel fluent now in the language of ghosts.

ACKNOWLEDGMENTS

When a soldier tries to simply spell a word, but can't, so breaks it into its individual letters: "with all his fac—, *with all his f-a-c-u-l-t-i-e-s intact*," this final line in J. D. Salinger's "For Esmé—With Love and Squalor," won't leave me. I have just spent three years in the company of ghosts. I question whether I have returned with all my fac— with all my faculties intact. I need them now, for this is a serious assignment, the acknowledgment of those whose contributions to this book won't be apparent to most readers.

My instincts tell me *start with your mother.* Salinger's short story was one of her favorite examples of the craft of writing. This is the lady who gave me a thirteen-pound dictionary for my college graduation. Her ghost in my ear: "Salinger meant 'faculties' as in senses. But look it up. It also means teachers."

I extend this idea to include my Deepdene Writers Workshop classmates. Their patience with my drafts of horse-themed stories is laudatory—all of us disciples of Johns Hopkins University memoir and fiction-writing instructor Margaret Osburn who, luckily for me, also likes horses.

Secret weapon to vet my unfinished lines: lawyer-turned-wordsmith Jay Merwin. He returns my submissions in two formats: redlined and clean. Very clean. He exercises restraint: "Don't overdo the ghost thing." I can't help it, Jay. They're everywhere in my head.

Page ix of Mom's thirteen-pound gift of words is entitled "Guide to the Use of the Dictionary." It's dry stuff: Main Entry, Pronunciation, Part-of-Speech. These are the fundamentals of language. When I began researching century-old documents foisted onto attic tables, I felt weak-kneed about the fundamentals of a new language: I needed a "Guide to the Use of Archives." On cue, Elizabeth Schaaf arrived fresh from her decades as archivist of the prestigious George Peabody Library in Baltimore. Two years into the three-year project of writing this book—and just as her Gaylord archival storage boxes began to impose order—Elizabeth slipped and fell at the bottom stairs to this old farmhouse. Some gravestones soften the finality of it all: ". . . Fell Asleep" on such-and-such a date. How I wish I could awaken Elizabeth.

To restore—to bring back to a former condition—that is the specialty of Coyle Studios in Baltimore, where John and Mary Lou Coyle, Brynne Devereaux, and Amy Meyer bring back the dead, putting a pulse in pictures of the departed. Photography was in its infancy when immigrants such as my ancestors landed in New York City, and thus every photo, by definition, is a rare photo. For negatives to be developed and preserved is to live once more. That Grandfather seldom smiled in photographs is belied by the light Coyle Studios finds in his eyes, the windows to his soul.

Acknowledge, as a verb, appears early in Mom's big book: "To understand, know." Acknowledgment, as a noun, is an expression of thanks. To all the horses of history, famous or not. How they enrich our lives with their mere being. Just think of the horses in the Wounded Warrior program, what they do for battle-fatigued veterans such as Salinger's hero, the way horses help us all face the world with our f-a-c-u-l-t-i-e-s intact.

ABOUT THE AUTHOR

Josh Pons won two Eclipse Awards for his journalism in *BloodHorse*, presented for best stories of the year in the sport of Thoroughbred racing. He is the author of two books published by Eclipse Press: *Country Life Farm: Three Years in the Life of a Thoroughbred Horse Farm* and *Merryland: Two Years in the Life of a Thoroughbred Training Farm.*

Pons joined *BloodHorse* upon graduation from the University of Virginia, where he majored in English. After three years as a journalist, he entered the University of Kentucky Law School, graduating in 1982, then returned to his family's Country Life Farm.

Professionally, he served as president of the Maryland Horse Breeders Association for six years and is currently president of the foundation responsible for the Maryland Horse Library and Education Center. He and his wife, Ellen, live in Fallston, Maryland, on Country Life, the oldest Thoroughbred farm in the state.